D1730320

Also by Anamika

French Lessons in Love...and some lessons in language too

Love in Fur Coats: Gifts from my animal companions

and...

Loving Now

Anamika

Cover design by Stephan Choiniere
Cover photo by Jennifer Goodrich
Author photo by Norman Seeff

Edited by Marty Hale and Laurel Airica

Special thanks: Irene Mink, Katerina Getchell, Greg Winters, Jennifer and Michael Goodrich, Steve Parrish

Formatted by Karen Richardson

Revised and updated version of
Into the Heart of the Beloved: A Romance with the Divine

More information at www.anamika.com

ISBN: 978-0-9908379-0-9

Loving Now / Anamika.

CONTENTS

preface

Last summer, while I was cleaning out my house in preparation to move, I came across a copy of a book I had written years ago. It describes the events that occurred during a powerfully transformative period of my life from 1984 to 1996.

Throughout that period, even though I had some gloriously elevating and earth-shaking experiences and realizations, I didn't predominantly live in Love as a state of being. Making that shift was extremely challenging for me because it required letting go of control on levels far deeper than I could ever have imagined at the time.

This book chronicles many different stages of development that I went through. For example, I had considered the end goal to be achieving "enlightenment." I mistakenly thought that this was a place at which one arrives having mastered perfection and constant bliss. Not only did I discover that this concept was inaccurate, I also came to understand that there really is no end goal. Each step is an invaluable part of an eternally unfolding process of getting to know, cherish and be oneself ever more fully and authentically.

Since we are always growing, learning, and expanding, I couldn't have imagined the richness that was yet to come through continually integrating and enlightening. I also can't imagine what's still to be revealed.

As I reread the old book, I reflected back upon the person I was with a tender smile. The differences in my perspectives then and now are very evident to me. Yet, I'm still the same person, in fact even more genuinely so—though paradoxically also quite different.

In reviewing my life, I see that my passion to know myself—and my fervent desire to live and create from an always expanding sense of self—were always there. They are the luminous thread that connects all of the events. What is vastly different now is how I experience myself as well as what I create from a new sense of self. I was evolving from seeking love, to falling in love, to knowing myself as Love, to Loving Now.

I am republishing the original book in an updated version. To distinguish clearly between then and now, I have included the original experiences in plain font, *and new commentary from my present perspective in italics. My inner voice is in quotation marks throughout. The experiences are true but I have given pseudonyms to the people involved and made them into fictitious characters.*

I continue to write about my life-changing adventures and realizations. These books are available on my website www. anamika.com. I offer these in honor of who we've been, of who we are now, and of who we're becoming.

May we cherish ourselves and each other with appreciation and tender compassion.

With love,
Anamika

introduction

If the Nazis came to the door what would I do? This question haunted my childhood. Would I faint? Would I run and hide? Would I resist even if it meant losing my life?

These questions were understandable given that I grew up in a Jewish household not too long after World War II. However, the intensity of my feelings surrounding this quandary and my desperation to know the answer seemed strange. There was no history of violence in my childhood. My family enjoyed a comfortable upper-middle class, Oyster Bay Cove, New York existence. We valued kindness. So my obsession with this Nazi issue had to come from somewhere else.

In attempting to find answers, I would conjure up various scenarios. In some, possessing super human strength, I defeated the Nazis' advances. In others, I bravely faced death at the hands of my captors. In others, I quaked in terror at the sight of their hard black boots and threatening guns.

After each of these ruminations I would be left in a state of great agitation and unrest because I truly didn't know what I would do if confronted in such a way. And so, the quandary continued.

Years later, as I reached through the veils of time in an altered state of consciousness, a vivid recollection of what seemed like a prior life made clear the reason for my childhood obsession with the Nazis. Finally, what seemed like an answer emerged. I was a fifteen-year old boy in Eastern Europe and one day the Nazis did indeed knock on the door. Although my stomach clenched as terror coursed through my veins, I opened the door and strategically positioned myself in such a way that my body offered what protection it could to shield my family. Courageously, I stood tall before the Nazis, lying to them that my family was not at home. I desperately hoped that the soldiers would believe my ruse and move on.

Instead, they viciously grabbed me and brutally clubbed me to death. Even after my skull was broken, they continued to pummel and kick me. My spirit hovered over my lifeless body in shock at what had happened, watching helplessly as the Nazis stormed the house. They dragged my struggling younger sister, parents and grandparents into the street, and threw them in a filthy truck to be hauled off to a concentration camp.

I was devastated beyond description. I had failed in my mission to protect those I loved most and I had failed to defeat the forces of darkness. In an attempt to rectify the situation, my spirit made a desperate effort to re-inhabit my brutalized body. Relatives in spirit turned me around and drew me toward the Light, away from my earthly existence. My heart was heavy. I had been determined to be a force of good, believing that it was my mission to save the world and fight the darkness.

From somewhere in the ethers a gentle soothing voice began to speak. "It is not necessary to win that fight. Forgive yourself for not being able to do what you thought you should. Winning a fight is not important. What is important is that you forgive yourself for not accomplishing what you thought you should. In so doing, you will attain a profound level of acceptance in which you re-evaluate your priorities and discover that you don't have to be other than who you are."

I realized that I could blend with the Light and know serenity. But I had felt like an utter failure because I had not been strong enough to accomplish what I had believed to be right. The comforting voice continued. "Who says you should have been able to defeat the soldiers? Why judge yourself so harshly? Who says that your limited perspective is the only reality? You can only find out if you move into a different state of being."

"I can't do that," I pleaded. "Some things are just unforgivable. I wasn't able to save my family and help defeat the forces of darkness. I need to go back to Earth and fulfill this mission. I cannot rest until I do."

"As you wish. However, if you want to come to peace, you will need a gift, one that will help you learn unconditional love and acceptance."

"Excellent," I exulted. "When do I begin?"

"It will require many years of life to reach a level of maturity sufficient to know yourself as one with this gift. In the meantime, be aware of when you misuse it for self-serving purposes.

"Eventually you will come to learn that the compassionate embrace of yourself as you are, including your darkness and your light, is actually what you are seeking, not conquering the dark. But, you'll need to discover this for yourself.

"You're going to forget this conversation for a time. You will not remember the gift I am giving you or anything about this interaction until you are able to transcend self-judgment sufficiently. At a certain stage in your development you will remember. So be it."

Of course, just as the voice said, I remembered none of this. My life was consumed by a nameless quest spurred on by a nameless angst. It was a desperate search for something that would relieve the ache and make me feel whole. Certainly there were days, even years of pleasure, accomplishment, and learning. By all accounts, I was extremely successful. Yet, something was missing.

A consuming yearning, a longing beyond all things persisted. Usually I placed the focus of this longing on a man. If I could just find the right man, not the one I was currently with, but that ultimate soul mate life partner, the One, then I could have the thirst quenched and the pain lifted.

If I wasn't focused on the man, it was the mission. Why am I here? What I am supposed to be doing? What's my true purpose and destiny?

My search for this these answers led me all over the planet. I explored high rocky terrain and eerily silent deserts. I delved deeply into my psyche, fearlessly searching, questioning, and probing. I would stop at nothing, leaving no stone unturned. I was relentless.

Despite the many insights accumulated through the search, the gaping black hole in my being persistently haunted me. Where is my man? When will we meet? Why am I here? What is my mission?

These questions never got answered in the way I was looking for, but something more important and real occurred. A significant turning point that helped me resolve these questions occurred when I met a man named Joffrey with whom I had honest and illuminating conversations.

In speaking with him, every belief I held dear was challenged. Every truth I had held as reality was exposed as limited. I got to strip naked my psyche, and to relinquish the self I had thought was me, removing shrouds of self-deception.

Given the magnitude of the shift in consciousness I was undergoing, there was much involved. Perhaps some go through this gracefully, but I can't say that was true of me. I felt tortured, manipulated, controlled and confused. I pleaded, demanded, raged, bargained, ranted, raved and sobbed my way through. I was certain that if only I had the right man and mission I would be just fine. Then, I would have that consummate Love. I thought my search was for a soul mate, for a purpose, for enlightenment. In truth, it was a search to know, to accept and to love myself.

This is the story of how my suffering gave way to miraculous grace during that period of my life. While my journey is distinctly personal, it is really the story of us all. As humans we have so much in common and at the same time we are all on our own uniquely beautiful journey of awakening. I hope my personal revelations further spark your heart's flame, the voice that speaks to you within, so it can burn ever more brightly as it illuminates the world.

CHAPTER 1

empty hole

I should have been on top of the world. By age 36, I had reached the pinnacle of my career and personal life. I was successful, highly accomplished and money flowed in abundance. I was involved with a caring and successful man who desired marriage. I had achieved what I thought I should. Yet something was missing.

I had been involved in the personal growth movement for twenty years. I had graduated from Wellesley College with a B.A. in Psychology, and then had gone on to a self-designed, non-traditional program in graduate school, to earn a Ph.D. in Psychology.

At nineteen, while still in college, I began my counseling practice. I discovered I had healing gifts as well as telepathic knowing. I was able to feel people's emotions and read their thoughts. I also had an ability to transmit energy that catalyzed spontaneous shifts of consciousness. It just flowed through my body when I cared about helping someone, expanding my consciousness and theirs. Yet I had no idea where it came from.

I had a booming psychotherapy and energy healing practice in Lexington, Massachusetts. After all of my schooling, I had trained for four more years in the Barbara Brennan School of Healing, which helped open up my budding gifts even further.

By now I had worked with thousands of clients and students and had traveled the world leading seminars on women's and men's liberation. Financially, I was in the top 1% of women on the planet.

Yet, I had a persistent feeling that something was missing. Whatever it was seemed like the most important thing. I had felt that way even as a child. As early as I could remember, I had been searching for that something.

I was looking for an inner feeling of fullness, an overwhelming Love and a radiant passion that forever eluded me. Instead, I was tormented by angst, disconnectedness, meaninglessness, and despair. I longed for the connection, oneness and union that would fill my being.

This angst persisted despite having a loving family and a powerful bond with my mother in particular. She and I shared a special relationship. We communicated perfectly with a mere glance or a knowing look. We read each other's thoughts and feelings to the detail. We were psychically attuned with an uncanny feeling that we had known each other for eons.

Even as an infant I felt that I was her mother as much as she was mine. It was as if we were one soul. My telepathic connection with her was present from the start. I could read her mind and she could read mine. Yet despite our extraordinary affinity, this connection wasn't enough. As much as I valued and relied on her love, I needed something that she could not give me.

I had a bottomless emptiness that my precocious maturity could not assuage. Despite moments of intense connectedness to something beyond the ordinary, I would fall back into the black hole. This greater awareness only magnified my disconnectedness and amplified my yearning for deeper communion.

So at 36, when my life appeared on the outside to be so successful, the feelings of angst inside became overwhelming. I was convinced that what I lacked was the right man and my true mission. I believed that the physical presence of my truest soul mate, and clarity about my life purpose, would fill the emptiness inside.

Searching for answers and craving healing balm, I approached psychics, healers, channels and mediums. I consulted with anyone who might have a clue as to where and when I would meet my soul mate and as to the nature of my mission. This proved to be a roller coaster ride with gut-wrenching swings.

Each time I thought that I was getting closer to answers my hopes would rally. They would then be dashed with devastating sorrow as the predictions invariably proved to be false. Gradually, disillusionment began to outweigh my desperation. I became disgusted and ceased consulting others about these questions.

One day, my trusted friend Gabriella called in a state of excitement. Gabriella is a few years older than me and we share the same birthday. A wonderful healer and intuitive, I had immediately been drawn to her as a soul sister when we had first met at a workshop in Vermont years prior. Now, she was calling to invite me to dinner at her house. She had met a fascinating man from South Africa who was coming to stay with her in Vermont for a few days and she wanted me to meet him. She thought he might have some perspective on some of my big life questions. Her description of him and his abilities was shrouded in mystery and she wouldn't tell me more than that she thought I would find him fascinating.

Despite the discouragement from my prior experiences consulting with 'seers' and healers, I felt compelled to meet him. In fact, I felt that I had to do so immediately. My impassioned intuitive response shouted that I could not indulge my despair this time.

After we scheduled a dinner at Gabriella's house for the very next evening, I became quite excited. This was despite a large degree of skepticism that warred with my previously thwarted, but now escalating hopes. My logic argued, "What are you so excited and nervous about? You're just having dinner with some South African man." However, I was surprised to find that I was shaken to the core. My entire body was vibrating with anticipation and fear. I sensed that this time would be different and that my two burning questions might actually be answered.

The next day, while driving a few hours to Gabriella's house, all of my worst fears rampaged in cacophonous disarray. I fantasized him coldly reprimanding me when I asked about my soul mate and my mission. "You have no soul mate. You're going to be alone for the rest of your life. Furthermore, you have no mission. So just get used to that!" It said something for the rattled state of my mind and nerves that I could only imagine this judgmental response.

With these depressing thoughts as companions, I approached Gabriella's house with the grace and enthusiasm of a robot—having finally numbed myself as a protection against further disappointment. Mechanically knocking on the door, I awaited what I believed could only be the inevitable demise of every hope and aspiration I had ever held dear.

After what felt to be an eternity, the door opened and there stood Joffrey. I was shocked. His appearance seemed all wrong. I thought I had no expectations of what he would look like. Yet I was seized by the irrational conviction that somehow he was supposed to look different than he did.

He was a tall, skinny unprepossessing man with pale white skin. His almost waist length blond hair hung loose. He had unfocused green eyes, which gazed at me blankly as he seemed to be drifting in and out of his body. It didn't seem possible that this seemingly disoriented man could possess any key to my well-being.

With this gloomy thought, I decided to put a brave front on the matter. Masking my nervousness, I marched into the foyer in a brusque manner, as if paying an official visit. Joffrey's initial awkwardness seemed to grow as if in response to my impersonal entrance. Perhaps my very presence was strangely disconcerting to him, I mused, feeling my slim thread of hope slipping away.

Joffrey indicated that I follow him into the kitchen where Gabriella was only beginning to make dinner. She said that while she made the preparations, he and I should go sit together in the living room. The shades were drawn and I could barely see him

in the dimly lit room. Two chairs had been carefully placed face to face next to a small table with a
burning candle. He motioned for me to take a seat
and asked me to take off my shoes. Then under
his breath he said some kind of prayer. I panicked.
"What is this, a séance?" I argued with myself as I
fought the urge to bolt from the room. "Get a hold
of yourself!" I demanded as I made an unsuccess-
ful effort to be more rational. My mind had a will
of its own. It went on, "If this guy was for real,
none of this craziness would be happening."

Somehow him saying a prayer reminded me of
what I categorized as religious nonsense. It was
something about safety, protection and intentions
for the highest good of all. Desperate for a measure of reassurance, I continued my silent mono-
logue, "Well, if he was as remarkable as Gabriella
had said, maybe the prayer was necessary after
all." Reassured by my analysis of the situation, I
took off my shoes as Joffrey had requested.

Right before he closed his eyes for a moment, he
looked at me in a very different manner than before. It was as if his eyes were looking through me.
The best way to describe it is that he looked like
he was seeing something that was invisible. His

look was penetrating, as if he were asking, "Don't I know you?" I remember feeling that he was scrutinizing my soul. This was a very uncomfortable moment. I felt more exposed than I had ever been in my life.

His visual probing lasted just a moment. Then he closed his eyes and as his breathing deepened his body began to slump. I thought he was taking a nap because odd sounds emanated from him. But then the air in the room softened palpably and became highly charged as if the fabric of our surroundings was shifting. Suddenly, I sensed a presence enter Joffrey's body and adjust itself to his form. At the same time I noticed that the shape of Joffrey's face and body were undergoing a transformation. His rather androgynous features were becoming much sharper and more boldly defined as if Joffrey were becoming a powerful persona.

By now, I was quivering with anticipation. I felt a strong recognition with this energy presence and was immediately at ease. Somehow I knew that its power was tempered by a great gentleness and a vast compassion. For the first time that day, I felt calm, safe and at peace.

Suddenly Joffrey bolted upright, opened his eyes, and started speaking. His voice was tender and understanding as he spoke to me of the dilemma of old soul's who are sensitive, and how challenging being on Earth can be, especially with the majority of humanity at a survival level of consciousness.

He acknowledged that even though I was dedicated to my path, my feeling of inner connectedness would come and go. He understood that I was confused as to why it didn't last and why my commitment to this inner focus had not brought me the kind of relationship and mission for which I was longing. He knew that I hoped it was because I was a late bloomer, but also that I was worried I might never bloom at all.

While he was talking I was trembling. This voice was addressing my heart directly. Yet it wasn't only his words that spoke to me. His presence emanated a kindness and a caring that was far beyond anything I had ever known. It was as if he was holding me in his arms against his chest. I felt that he knew me better than I knew myself. He accepted me completely, both the good and the bad. He knew my dreams, my desires, and what my soul was all about.

How did he know me? Despite my lingering mental agitation, on some profound level I felt like I had come home. Nothing looked the way I thought it should, but somehow that ceased to matter. He reassured me that old souls do tend to bloom late, like exquisite flowers whose beauty and scent lasts for hundreds of years once they finally blossom.

When our communion was complete, there was a long silent pause in which Joffrey's body began to slump again. During this pause, I felt the gentle etheric energy depart. Gradually, I sensed another presence occupying Joffrey's body. It was strongly masculine and earthy.

Again Joffrey's body bolted upright. He rubbed his eyes, shook his head vigorously, then grunted, looking around the living room. I was amazed at the change in Joffrey's appearance. He seemed squat, with a large belly and a jowly face. Incredibly, he seemed to be wearing a Native American headdress. When he began to speak, it was with a thick, gravely, voice. He introduced himself as a Native American Chief. He didn't mention his tribe.

Almost immediately I began to feel a pressure in the center of my chest and a swirling around my heart. "There's something happening to my heart right now. What is that?" I asked.

He told me that it was Yeshua, the man later called Jesus by the Romans, doing a healing on my heart. He went on to inform me that I had spent a lot of time with Yeshua.

I was incredulous. This didn't seem possible. I had always rejected any notion of the religious figure Jesus. I felt no need for a savior and he had no relevance to my life. In addition, I had always found the very sound of the name Jesus to be hard and grating. It had never occurred to me that I might have known a real person with the ancient Hebrew name Yeshua, which sounded melodious.

Surprised that I had any desire to speak with him, I heard myself asking, "Can Yeshua speak with me?"

He assured me that Yeshua as well as other Masters who had been on this Earth could and would come and speak with me eventually. They were interested in supporting all those who were opening to embrace the Light for awakening and to deepen in their awareness of God/Goddess/All-That-Is.

This fit into my notion of my mission. Even though I didn't understand much, I had a burning desire to further awaken and to help humanity do the same.

The Chief then paused and took a long breath. To my great surprise, he expressed his personal love for me and his words were filled with great emotion. I couldn't tell if this was some kind of universal Love he was expressing or something more personal from some other era. But I didn't have time to ruminate upon his startling admission, because as he spoke, I felt delicious warmth penetrating my heart in the place it yearned to be touched. He said nothing else other than expressing his sadness in having to leave, but assured me we would be together again in different ways.

I wondered what his mysterious message meant. How would we be together? What different ways?

Before I could ask him, his energy began leaving Joffrey's body. For a moment the Chief appeared before me as a huge being of golden white light radiating the most beautiful glow I had ever seen. I gasped, overcome with awe and longing. He lifted me up and drew me into his light. I began to sob as pain welled up and tears of gratitude spilled down my cheeks. This is it! This is the Love I have been looking for! I don't want it to ever end, I exulted, utterly transfixed.

Gradually, the Chief's light faded, but I maintained my euphoria. Suddenly, with a lurch and a start, Joffrey opened his eyes and was unceremoniously back in his body with no recollection of anything that had transpired.

I glanced down at my watch. We had been sitting together for an hour, but seemed both timeless and only 10 minutes long. I could hear Gabriella still in the kitchen making dinner. While Joffrey hadn't directly answered my two burning questions, strangely at that moment, while in the experience of Love, it didn't matter. Those questions were the furthest things from my mind.

As Joffrey's eyes came into focus, he saw me still in the throes of my ecstatic experience with the Chief. For a brief moment he exhibited none of the initial awkwardness he had when we first beheld each other. His eyes clearly indicated that he too was profoundly moved. Sometime later he told me that at that moment he became aware that there was a deep, lasting connection between us.

It had been there for eons. It seemed we had been together consistently in many different kinds of relationships throughout the centuries.

The eternal bond I felt at that moment was not only with Joffrey personally, because I didn't know him, but more with the energy coming through him. I didn't realize that his personal energy was still blended with that higher vibratory energy, and that he was to be an integral part of my journey as well.

This was my first experience of specific beings like the Chief, with their own personalities, blended with a person's energy. Up until that time, when I would merge with All, it was an undifferentiated state of oneness I would experience.

My experience with the energy of the Chief was so compelling it was like a magnet. I would try to recreate the sensations of Love we had entered into together when I was alone again with my eyes closed. It was the beginning of learning to access dimensions of consciousness other than ordinary reality by choice.

At this stage, even though I was looking outside of myself for this great Love, my real search was for union. I couldn't yet consistently sense that I was already connected in that union, so I looked for some kind of large presence who would be the source of that Love. I couldn't consistently yet access it within me. It was like a child looking for a loving parent.

As a child, although I had touched upon Love many times, as any young person does, I had predominately looked to my parents for human love. My parents were both kind-hearted people, but damaged in different ways. My mother was caring, intuitive and creative, but extremely dominating and controlling. My father was also very intelligent and multi-talented, but emotionally withdrawn and unavailable. Even thought my mother was very perceptive about other people, she wasn't very self-aware, while by contrast my father liked to understand his internal landscape. As a result of his introspection, years later he apologized to me for his emotional withdrawal. But my early negative imprints were of an emotionally absent father and of a mother who was a bully. This was a source of great pain to a little girl who adored her mommy and daddy.

Growing up, it seemed to me that had my parents had done it "right" I would feel fulfilled. I became angry at them, angry at myself assuming I must have done something wrong, and eventually withdrawn too.

Later, in working with thousands of people, I saw that even those who had more fulfilling parent/child relationships were still searching for something more. I realized that no matter how wonderful or terrible our human relationships were, they weren't ultimately the source of our happiness or pain. That came from within, and our parents were the cause of our happiness or pain only from a child's perspective. A more self-responsibly mature perspective showed me that our parents were a mirror of our own often unconscious beliefs and not the cause. They were the actors in our own play.

Eventually, I came to the liberating and empowering realization that my own connectedness was something that I could consciously choose instead of looking for it out there. In the process of learning to live in the awareness of that connectedness, this experience with Joffrey was one of many meaningful experiences that led me deeper into that union. So, in this first encounter with Joffrey, the eternal bond I felt was with this presence called the Chief, who seemed to exist only outside of me. I didn't yet fully realize that this presence was both outside of and also within me. In fact, he was part of me and I was part of him. At this stage, I couldn't reliably feel this Love within myself so I perceived myself as separate from it.

When I felt separate, I kept looking for my daily experiences to fill the emptiness inside. Like an addict, I would get a temporary 'fix' from my caring interactions with people, but the hole still remained. It was a persistent emptiness.

I couldn't understand why I didn't derive much fulfillment from ordinary worldly pleasures. I thought I should be able to fill the hole once and for all from a source of pleasure.

I did have an intellectual awareness that true, enduring contentment could only come from my own inner spiritual nature. But I wasn't feeling it. While I derived deep joy from learning more about myself and about the true nature of reality, I was uncertain how to access it and find further inner fulfillment. I didn't yet understand how to reliably tap into my own inner resonances and feel them vibrate within me. It seemed like it happened spontaneously to me once in a while by chance.

CHAPTER 2

cosmic preoccupation

Something changed in me after that first encounter with Joffrey. I was consumed by the desire to feel the vitality and affirmation of life that the energies offered. This desire gave my previously nameless quest a name and a direction. Although my life was full and busy, I could think of nothing else but the chance to see Joffrey again.

Until I met the energetic presence that called himself the Chief, I had been filled with an aching emptiness despite all the blessings I had in my life. I went through life feeling alone. The few glimmers of joy and connection I had momentarily experienced over the years with Spirit had been fleeting and haunting contrasts to the constant, low-grade despair that plagued me.

I now realized that I had always had a connection with those energies, and in fact they had always been my best friends silently whispering to me from within. With a gentle pressure, their unseen force had guided my movements. They provided a strong sense of inner knowing. If I became indecisive or confused it was their loving influence that impressed me with where to go and what to do. I had the same feeling with them now as when I was a child.

As a child, I called this presence 'Nature.' I found hints of that connection when in solitude. These moments often occurred when I was alone among the tall oaks in the woods surrounding our house, or lying comfortably on the wave-lapped sand by the seashore. As I lay on my back and fell upward into the sky, I expanded through the clouds into infinity and felt one with All.

However, I wasn't aware of the presence of Nature all of the time. When the spirit of Nature came to me, it would make its presence known by a feeling of great expansiveness in which I was quite empathic. I could sense other people's feelings and telepathically read their thoughts.

Nature was so attuned to me that it seemed prescient. It was as if it knew what I needed before I did. Because of Nature, I seemed to possess an awareness of other dimensions of reality. Somehow I knew that there was more depth and possibility around us than appeared in ordinary life. These other dimensions informed and guided me.

As a child in school, I couldn't relate to petty childish squabbles. Ordinary childhood interests held no significance for me, as if I was called by something much bigger going on than we realized. I often found myself wanting to shake other children at school and say, "Wake up! Don't you see? Aren't you interested in something more real? There's so much more to life than what we can see."

There was a tremendous contrast between the limited focus of daily life and the beauty that I sensed within and all around. It was as if Nature was constantly reminding me that there was more richness to life than what the ordinary was offering the young child that I was. This painful contrast strangely insured that I would not stop seeking the connectedness I so loved. I wasn't content with the intermittent access I had. I wanted more. I craved its delicious, powerful essence. I yearned to dissolve in its ecstatic, boundless passion.

Given this cosmic preoccupation, being on Earth felt like I had been conscripted to walk through a trivial play, and one that I knew too well. There was no mystery, no frontier at this stage; it was yet to come. I couldn't understand why I was required to conduct my affairs at what seemed like a snail's pace. I didn't yet understand the beauty of the play and importance of slowing down. So while rejecting life as it was, I was longing for something better to come. I had great hope that the next act of this play held the promise of a magnificent resolution.

Nature was my best companion, always counseling patience to my impetuous, eager spirit. In connecting with Nature, I would let go of my daily concerns, slow down, and expand into oneness. This still, slow pace taught me how to just be, feel and experience.

Now it was the beings speaking through Joffrey that were teaching me a new level of connectedness. In connecting with them, somehow their energy had reached through my despair and grabbed my heart. Miraculously, I didn't feel alone anymore. I finally felt like I had come home. It was as if I had found my long lost family and dearest friends. The exhilarating passion I felt was what I had always thought I would feel with a man. It was a taste of the great Love for which I had been searching.

The Chief's energy was direct and potent, like liquid gold pulsing through my veins. Through his energetic embrace, I felt all of creation dancing within me in sublime lovemaking. My entire body pulsed and tingled with wave after wave of exultation and rapture. This would happen all over again every time I slowed down and focused on him.

When I left that state, the deep abyss of aloneness and separation inside would be less tolerable than ever. All I wanted was to have that great Love be my constant companion. I determinedly vowed that I would do whatever it took, even walk through fire, to have this Love always.

As I made this vow, it was fortunate that I didn't know the arduous challenges that lay ahead. If I had, I'm not sure I would have been able to muster the commitment to carry on. My rapturous experience was actually a preview, a tantalizing appetizer that kept me going as I slogged through the wilderness of despair for many years to come. It was a gradual process of moving from one way of being—one paradigm—to another.

Unbeknownst to me, my progress would require that I relinquish firmly entrenched beliefs. I was riddled by a lack of self-worth to the point of violent self-hatred, which I had masked under the guise of superiority. Both thinking I was less than or more than left me isolated and separate. I didn't realize that to feel that sublime quality of Love consistently within me required that I cherish every part of myself completely, including the parts that felt less than or more than. This quest would be an extended odyssey in which I would have to examine and accept parts of myself that both frightened and repulsed me, as well as parts that pleased and delighted me. I would get to face and embrace everything.

I became aware of one such uncomfortable part after seeing Joffrey for the second time a year later. The pull to see him again was so strong, that when Gabriella informed me that he had returned to visit her in Vermont again, I rushed to her house.

As I entered the house, he mistakenly called me Alexandra. We were both startled and surmised it meant something significant. He reflected upon it for a moment and said that it was not Alexandra, but that I carried the kind of issues as did Alexander as in Alexander the Great. In Alexander's story, Joffrey went on, he himself had been like the person who was Alexander's best general and closest friend.

I told Joffrey that I had been aware of a sense of being a powerful man who had conquered much of the world—and in the process had killed, raped, burned, pillaged, and plundered. I had remembered the actions, but had not recalled his identity. Now he was informing me that this memory was from the life of Alexander the Great, one of history's movers and destroyers. I also knew that in a drunken brawl and fight, Alexander had killed his best general and closest friend.

Joffrey looked me deeply in the eyes and suddenly scenes from Alexander's lifetime surfaced, flooding into my awareness like unwelcome guests. The guilt, shame, and sorrow at what he had done were devastating. As I realized that all of those feelings were part of me, I sobbed inconsolably. Sitting there in Gabriella's living room, after several hours, I could begin to forgive myself and mentally ask for forgiveness from those I personally had injured with those same uncaring attitudes.

It challenged me sorely to find compassion for myself, or anyone who had played the oppressor or perpetrator role. In that role, we had done such vile acts to countless "innocent victims" who seemed to have done nothing to deserve our draconian intervention in their lives. It seemed that we deserved nothing but opprobrium, revilement and condemnation. I heaped the most severe punishment upon myself in the form of self-criticism.

Somehow, in reviewing these imagined scenes of Alexander's life, I sensed that more was required of me than just regret about this behavior. I realized that I must find compassion for the conquering part of Alexander. While his intentions were to spread culture and learning, his methods were brutal.

Yet, Alexander was also part of the callous mentality of the day. I also had the impression that he was a severely wounded and insecure man. I could feel the enormity of his inner pain. It was as huge as the empire he created.

Compassion for his victims seemed easier to find than compassion for him. However, through my remorse, I came to see that his actions were, in part, a result of his lack of self-worth in which he was trying to prove himself to the world over and over and over again. Yet, he could never win out over his own self-doubt. I could relate to that need. Knowing myself, I surmised that he would not have hurt another being except from his own deep pain. This did not excuse his actions but I found compassion for his humanity—and my own in the process.

I felt kindred to this brilliant, murderous conqueror. Thus, reflecting on him—and dealing with what came up for me—helped heal a deep level of self-contempt. I realized that all of us had done it all and played every role. I saw the victims and perpetrators mutually attracted to each other, each playing their own part to perfection. In this larger sense nobody was a victim of any situation or of another person.

This recognition freed me from the guilt, but not from a deep sense of responsibility for my actions. Without the guilt, however, I could more easily forgive my mistakes, ignorance, and lack of awareness. I softened into a gentle compassion for my imperfections and those of others. For the moment, it was all okay.

CHAPTER 3

coming to earth

Weeks later, an imagined story of Joan of Arc surfaced when Gabriella came to my house for an afternoon visit. When she asked, "Did you know that today is Joan of Arc's birthday?" her question shot through me like a jolt of electricity. Without any warning I felt so faint that I would have fallen to the ground had Gabriella not caught me.

In the midst of this swoon, I began to smell burning flesh, feel hot searing flames engulfing her body, and hear her hair burning like straw. As I re-experienced her horror of being burned at the stake it was as if I could hear her screaming, "I love God! I love God! You can kill my body, but you cannot kill my spirit! You can't make me stop loving God!"

I sensed that a crowd around her was agitated and grief-stricken. She was thankfully pulled out of her charred body by a guiding spirit and merged with the Light, floating freely away from the scene.

Gabriella held me gently in her arms and stroked my hair as I was seeing these scenes until I returned to the present. Reliving Joan's adoration of God was overwhelmingly beautiful. She had been willing to do whatever it took to honor this—even to the point of being consumed by fire. Yet maybe she had played the martyr too? I realized that while I wanted to do whatever it took to awaken, it was becoming less and less attractive to do it by playing martyr, victim, persecutor or savior.

After this experience with Gabriella, memories of other archetypes began to surface. I remembered dwelling between dimensions and making the choice to enter this life. I had met with advisors in spirit with whom I drew up a loose blueprint in preparation for my return to Earth.

I remembered being conceived. There was a burst of light and a tractor beam connecting my spirit with my parents. Our three energies came together creating an illuminated matrix that allowed me to come through as their daughter. I felt myself being squeezed down a vortex whose tremendous force seemed to suck me through its funnel to create the appearance of matter.

Cell by cell, I grew a body. Floating peacefully in the amniotic fluid of my mother's womb, I recall perceiving the many biochemical fluctuations that occurred. I was keenly aware of my mother's circadian rhythms. There were different tonalities of light as night broke into day and day folded back into night. I could sense my mother's emotions, feeling when she was happy or afraid. I was aware of her interactions with other people, especially with my father.

When the time came to leave my warm, watery home, I was not at all certain I was ready to go. I had grown quite comfortable in the warmth my mother had provided. Despite my hesitancy, the force and pressure of her contractions began. After momentarily digging in my heels in resistance, I realized that these contractions were the embodiment of something familiar. They were part of the forces of Nature, which were much greater than I. Resistance to such a force, which has it's own intelligence, was futile. Further convinced by the power of the next contraction's squeeze, I surrendered to being born.

As I entered into the world, I was unexpectedly thrust onto a cold metallic platform and could hear another baby screaming. I thought, "Oh, no, not this again! Not another life on Earth! What have I done?" I realized the enormity of my decision to return to Earth and for an instant was convinced I had made a catastrophic mistake.

Then I felt my mother's love beaming upon me. She was clearly communicating, "Oh, I remember you! We will again be the best of friends!" Relieved to be with her, I relaxed and expressed in return, "I'm so happy to be with you, too."

That initial interaction set the tone for our entire future relationship. We were indeed the best of friends, a constant source of alliance and support for each other. We never wavered from this foundational truth, despite the many difficulties we faced and worked through with each other over the years.

In the moments following my birth, her waves of love suddenly shifted. Now angry thoughts about my father coursed through her. He had become entangled in Columbus Day Parade traffic and was delayed by several hours. By the time he arrived at the hospital she was seething with resentment. She turned to me once more and telepathically communicated, "You're my deepest love. You don't let me down like he does. Your father is my companion, but if I had to choose right now between the two of you, it would be you."

Her message both pained and delighted me. I knew the absoluteness of her love; it provided comfort and security. But I recoiled at the comparison of her love for my father and me. I felt burdened by the enormous responsibility I felt in the face of her need.

I could feel my father at a distance, stuck in traffic. He was lost in a wash of self-recrimination and inadequacy for not anticipating congestion on a holiday and seeking an alternate route. I could feel him reaching to me through his self-judgment, attempting to make contact. This event set the template for my relationship with my father as well. It was one of reaching for connection and almost making it, but not quite. My heart sank, "I've just arrived and this is a complicated mess already! I'm not sure I can handle all of this!"

When I was older, my mother and I often lounged on our family's floral print overstuffed chairs discussing life. Once I asked her, "What do you recall of my birth? Would you describe it to me in as much detail as possible?" She replied without hesitation, "When I first laid eyes on you I was delighted and thought, "Oh, I remember you! We will again be the best of friends!" There was another baby crying in the room, and I was enraged by your father's delay." We were both amazed when her memories verified every detail of what I had recalled!

She went on to say that as I was growing up she never had to correct, instruct or explain anything to me. She didn't have to say, "The stove is hot, don't touch it." Somehow I already knew. Somehow all of that circuitry was in place as if I had already been here before so many times that I didn't need to re-learn the basics. It was as if I just wanted to get childhood over with so that I could focus on the spiritual evolution that required so many years of reflection and development.

Despite this clarity of telepathic connection, I still absorbed my mother's matrix and energetic programming. Much of it reflected my own beliefs that I brought with me into this life.

Over time, I put all of my own beliefs—as well as my reactions to my parents and others—under a magnifying glass. It was symptomatic of the self-examination that my dialogues with Joffrey would also demand. I had to relinquish my "reality," being right, being in control, and doing it my way. I was constantly challenged to release all of the beliefs that I held dear. There were no assurances, no guarantees, and no fine print. I could escape nothing and got to own all that I liked and all that I disliked as part of me.

Despite the fear of losing control, I knew I had to maintain a dialogue with my inner voice, no matter what doubts or fears arose. With that presence, I felt most trusting and at home. At each step, I chose to follow that voice.

After my second experience with Joffrey, and resolving the energy Alexander the Great represented, I yearned incessantly for another encounter. As the months went by, my impatience did not diminish. To the contrary, his absence was its own form of agony.

CHAPTER 4

risking trust

It was almost six months before Joffrey came back to Vermont to visit Gabriella. She enjoyed having him come visit, and generously hosted his sessions with other people. At long last, the moment of my third visit arrived. Joffrey was in the living room as before, in one of the two big armchairs facing each other. He followed the same ritual as the first time. He lit the candle, which sat on the little table, asked me to take off my shoes while he said the same prayer. This time I endured the ritual itself with more patience, but was holding my breath to see what would happen this time.

As Joffrey closed his eyes, I experienced feeling one with the energies again. This time a gentle voice with an East Indian accent came to address me. He introduced himself as my Master Guide, the one with the greatest access to me right now. Then, in a pointed and deliberate way he said that he was not my Master Teacher, just my Master Guide. He pierced me with a mysteriously significant look when he mentioned my Master Teacher, then lightened up again as he asked if there was any particular spirit with whom I would like to speak.

My heart leapt as I asked to speak with the Chief so that I could bask in the warmth of that great Love once again. My Master Guide left abruptly after a gentle nod and suddenly I was with the Chief again. For openers, he wanted me to guess what subject he was avoiding discussing with me. I knew exactly what he was referring to.

"Relationships," I blurted out.

Then, as would often prove to be the case, he avoided addressing the subject directly by asking another question. His roundabout approach this time was to ask about my personal happiness.

"No, I can't say that I am happy. I still have a desperate longing inside, a burning desire for Love."

I was hoping he would tell me when my soul mate would come, but much to my dismay he had a teaching to bring to the table, not a concrete answer or psychic prediction. Part of me just wanted some man to give me the love, and didn't want more spiritual lessons about accepting all of my feelings.

But this time, after counseling me to accept all of my feelings rather than pushing them away, he indicated that we had known each other deeply at a certain period in time. This piqued my interest greatly, but more than that, he wouldn't reveal.

The Chief's teaching style was incremental, dropping hints and clues like bread crumbs to draw me forward. He only revealed what he knew I could handle at the time. He was accurate in his assessment that I tended to push away from my upsets rather than gently embracing all of my feelings. I couldn't see how this approach of self-acceptance would allow me to experience Love. I was still trying to perfect myself sufficiently to 'earn' it from another person out there.

I was hardwired to fight and strive for what I wanted rather than to soften and open into that Love inside of me. I didn't understand that instead of feeling, I was fighting to grab something or to push away from something. It was a perpetual push/pull. Like a beach ball in the ocean, the more vigorously I fought to grab the ball, the more I actually caused it to move away from me.

I didn't yet understand that life was a creation of my own inner beliefs and consciousness. I thought life happened to me and that I was a victim of it. Thus, I was always angry, frustrated and impatient when I couldn't control the ocean to bring me the beach ball. I spent years feeling angry that the ocean of life didn't flow the way I wanted it to and wasn't under my control.

Later I learned that by entering the resonance I wanted to feel within myself—such as Love—it would elegantly create my outer reality in ways that delighted and surprised me beyond what I could make happen by force. It took me years to surrender into and stand in those resonances sufficiently to create effortlessly and magically from their beauty.

After that simple but powerful teaching he was gone, leaving me nearly breathless from the interaction with his energy. Another presence entered Joffrey's body, changing his face to that of a very young, almost angelic presence with a high feminine voice. She, too, wanted to play a game by having me guess who she was.

"An angel? I ventured.

Not quite, but close. She was a seraph, with a different role than an angel. She came as a herald to help prepare me to experience a more direct connection with Love. Like the Chief, she wanted me to first learn to connect with my own inner energy. She wanted to help illuminate my own inner radiance until I was glowing with my own Light. She promised that as I did, I would experience more lusciousness and that I would attract others to me with ease.

Before she left, she made one other suggestion, which floored me. She wanted me to get to know God intimately, not only like a best friend but also like a lover.

When she suggested that God wanted that with me, I interrupted with exasperation. "I don't even know who or what God is. I don't even believe in God. What is God?"

She wouldn't answer this conceptually. The only way I could know, she told me, would be directly through my own personal love affair with God. She really emphasized the word 'personal' when discussing how God relates to each person on a distinctly personal level. I got the unmistakable sense from her that every person's relationship with God is their own personal romance.

I was stunned by her words. "How do you know that's actually going to happen for me?"

She explained to me that the role of heralds is for that exact purpose—to herald the coming of that experience.

"So what I need to do now is to develop my own personal and intimate relationship with a God I don't know?" I asked incredulously. "

That's it exactly!" She sounded genuinely excited, like a little child.

I didn't know what on Earth she was talking about. I meant it when I said I didn't believe in God. I was raised a reformed Jew and many of the members of our synagogue were atheists. We were Jews by tradition, but not by religion. We believed there was no God. Our "religion" was a cultural and political statement of an oppressed people who were determined to be liberated and sustain their homeland. We had been brought up to believe that people needed to depend on their rational abilities to create the sort of life that produced happiness. We believed that life after death was not possible. All we had was here and now. The intangible did not exist.

While I was growing up, our family had scoffed at those who practiced religious beliefs. Regular attendance at Temple was viewed as superstitious nonsense that was beneath us. As we listened to our religious churchgoing neighbors pay homage to their God, a gray-haired man in the sky, and to Jesus who was their savior, we would roll our eyes as if saying, "What ignorance! How could they believe this nonsense?" We were an intellectual group concerned with empowering ourselves, not using religion as a crutch.

We had strength of will and an enormity of pride that was born of our ability to survive. We survived the pogroms. We survived the holocaust. We survived millennia of persecution and now it's up to us. We can't sit idly and wait for others to insure our freedom. We must take charge of our own lives and make sure we are never persecuted again. This perspective was the food of my early years.

In stark contrast, now I had this Seraph telling me I needed to have a more intimate relationship with "God." Needless to say I was appalled and repulsed. The idea seemed vile and despicably weak. Nevertheless, inexplicably I found myself opening to this suggestion. For some reason, I decided to act on faith that there was a "God" who wanted an intimate relationship with me, as long as I didn't have to really believe it!

I could sense that my need to aggressively and powerfully control my life and be fiercely independent was really a desperate effort to protect myself, to find safety. What I had vaingloriously described as 'controlling my destiny' only showed that I actually felt overwhelmed and powerless. I realized that these atheistic beliefs had contributed to the feelings of isolation and alienation that had tormented my childhood. I had both sensed and denied that there was more to life than our rational, material world.

What I didn't realize at the time is that when I tried to take control, I was in a fight with myself. By rejecting and judging whatever I was experiencing in each moment, I created a wall of discomfort.

I was pushing away from my own experience in each moment, and was instead looking for something else. I was suffering from wanting life to be different than it was—no matter how it was. It was never good enough and I was never satisfied.

I wasn't yet embracing each moment as it was. I didn't trust the movement and flow of my own experiences to guide and expand me. I kept fighting against my own soft inner flow of feelings to try to be in control and make something else happen according to what I thought should be happening. Only when I did allow my real emotions to flow through my heart would I truly feel them rather than trying to control them. Then, I would be happy and at peace, no matter what was occurring and what I was feeling. This would happen spontaneously during times when I was experiencing great beauty in music or nature, or when working with a client.

I began to realize how strong the desire was to stay in control, to do it my way, and to get it right. I thought that my way would produce the results I was looking for. I was trying hard to follow the set of rules I was taught should produce the desired results.

Thus, I was faithfully giving my power to the limited yet prevailing world perspective that was embedded in my mind. I was not yet reliably and consistently accessing the natural flow of my heart, even though I was searching for that freedom.

During this period, I was starting to experience more and more moments of expansion into Love, Beauty and Freedom. I would touch that ever-present aspect of myself and enter its flow. In this state, I could see through new eyes and feel a delicious reality. It was what I had been contacting since childhood and I was touching it now in a more beautifully and richly complex way.

This was the terrible contradiction within me. I had been denying what I had instinctively known to be true, the glorious realms beyond the linear. In these dimensions of reality was the profound harmony and serenity that I found on Earth only when communing with my own multi-dimensional consciousness.

I was able to expand beyond my rational, analytical beliefs because of the relationship that I had had with Nature throughout my childhood. Nature's gentle comforting presence had prepared me to accept dialogue with beings in spirit as a more intense, articulate form of itself. To me at this stage, Nature was not God. It was simply part of material reality. Therefore, it wasn't that great a stretch to accept multi-dimensional consciousness without addressing the greater theological and existential questions regarding the existence of God.

I drew a false distinction between Nature and God. I could only face the vulnerability inherent in relinquishing control

and opening to more expansive consciousness
time. As with everything, it was an incremente
took time to integrate and embody. Otherwise, ...
only been a new set of beliefs or ideas. I wanted to truly live
from a new reality, not just acquire a new set of beliefs. To
me that was the difference between a new intellectual spiri-
tuality and an embodied new state of being.

It didn't take long to find something to test my newfound trust. I discovered I was pregnant! This news came as an unexpected shock because I had been told at eighteen that I had a slight hormonal imbalance and would never become pregnant. In addition, I had just ended my relationship with this particular man and emphatically did not want a child, especially not with him!

I immediately set an appointment for an abortion but was horrified at the prospect. I didn't object to abortion on moral grounds. Rather, the thought of it stimulated distant "memories" of physical violation such as rape and mutilation. My hope was to miscarry rather than abort.

Alighting upon what I thought was a clever idea, I decided that if this God I was learning to trust wanted to have a relationship with me, God could

⌐ something to prove it. I was still referencing an omnipotent energy outside of myself who was bigger than I was and to whom I was giving my power. "Okay, Source," I demanded defiantly, "If you want an intimate relationship with me, here's what I want you to do. As I need a concrete sign that you exist, here's the deal: I need a miscarriage on August 31st."

Having issued this ultimatum, I had only ten days to experience pregnancy. During this time, I allowed myself to experience the soft, rosy aura pregnant women exude. I was surprised to find a great desire to commune with the spirit of the fetus growing within me, for I thought I had just wanted to get this over with as quickly as possible. Just as I had done as a fetus inside my own mother, I was able to communicate telepathically with this spirit, but this time from a mother's perspective. We fell deeply in love, rendering the ten days bittersweet with the knowledge that the connection in this form would soon end.

Several days before the scheduled abortion, I sensed the spirit withdrawing. The gentle communion stopped. In its place was a void, a melancholy emptiness. This quickly dissolved into pain, a stark contrast to the delicious warmth in which we had been steeping.

As the day of reckoning drew closer, I began to doubt what little faith I had placed in this external God. Plunging into despair, I was certain that I had been a complete fool to set up a ridiculous test only to prove to myself that there was no God.

August 31st arrived. No blood. As the day wore on, I became increasingly panicked. Would I miscarry or not? Would I need the abortion I had scheduled? Evening arrived and still there was no release. I collapsed in tears of despair on the cold tile of the bathroom floor. I shook my fist at the heavens screaming, "You see, I knew it! There is no God!"

Then suddenly, without warning, there was a torrent of blood as if someone had heard my tortured prayer. At that moment, I was as shocked as I had been when I found out I was pregnant!

Collecting myself, I got up from the cold tile, cleaned myself off, then lay down gingerly on my bed to rest. The cramping had begun. I drifted in and out of sleep as the contractions of the miscarriage continued throughout the night. When morning broke, I went to the doctor to be examined. She confirmed that I was indeed miscarrying, but was in no danger.

Simultaneously overwhelmed with grief, loss and gratitude, I sensed a warm energy gently comforting me. Between tears I sensed the baby's spirit now embraced by other spirits. The warm energy informed me that the spirit had held no intention of ever being born, but had desired practice crossing between the worlds. I had gotten to act on faith in this situation and to accept what was occurring without knowing the outcome in advance. Quite an exercise in trust!

After this experience I felt a deeper connection with Source than ever before. I began to understand that my every day experiences were my spiritual path. My life was not something outside of me. The pregnancy experience was my first real test of this new perspective, and it was a mighty one, indeed, as I was dealing with life and death. As it turned out well, my trust in the existence of God increased.

Even though at this stage I was putting my trust in a God outside myself who was more powerful than me—like a perfect, supreme daddy—through this experience I committed myself further. I was taking another step forward in challenging my old beliefs and opening to greater discoveries of my connectedness to All. I wanted not to believe in anyone's concept of "God" but to experience the truth of reality beyond the ordinary.

I decided to continue on faith that something called God existed. I became more willing to challenge my feelings of separation from union with this Oneness. I wanted to find out for myself what the Seraph had meant about what building an intimate relationship with "My Beloved."

CHAPTER 5

surrendering

My newfound trust precipitated a considerably stronger flow of energy as I worked with my clients. My intuitive and healing capabilities were enhanced and I was able to effect more profound interventions as I allowed the unseen energies to flow through me. For example, a new client arrived from the neighboring state of New Hampshire. She described her illness and the first words that seemingly forced their way out of my mouth was to go see Dr. Grayson, a man I had never heard of. She said that someone had just given her his name that morning.

Then she decided to ask me about a woman friend in China and about her dog who had crossed over. When all of the information I passed along was accurate, I had to go further past my doubts to understand that we are all interconnected beyond space and time and those realms were as real and accessible as "concrete" matter.

Even though this is common knowledge now, it was relatively new to me at that time. I was engaged in a process of learning to trust the perceptions that came from my senses beyond the ordinary.

I was evolving beyond rational atheism. Throughout this evolution, doubt played a prominent role. Despite the frequent experiences of Source in my life, I wasn't able to simply accept these new perspectives without fear and doubt. I thought I should be able to, and didn't realize the beauty of fear and the presence of insecurity as a part of the process.

It was all new, and nagging reservations persisted. I had to constantly remind myself that the glorious feelings of rightness that pervaded my life were symptomatic of my new connectedness. Even though I couldn't prove it, I knew in my heart of hearts that what was occurring was wonderful and that consciousness was real.

Day after day I practiced standing in the truth that this intensified energy I was feeling was Source, and was supporting me through these serious doubts. The continual transformation of doubt into further trust was part of the process each step of the way.

The more I opened to the energies coursing through me, the more I trusted them. Since I couldn't comfortably call them God, I called them Source, Spirit or the Energies, much in the way I called this force Nature as a child. I was learning to trust that the Energies were always there and would do the work effortlessly and more elegantly than I could. I didn't have to do it all through control. I could open beyond that.

As I relaxed the fearful survival clench in my belly and attuned to the Energies, they flowed strongly and guided me. It became quite evident that they were stronger and wiser than the little personality "I" was. Blended with them, I was elevated to my limitless, infinite Self. Yet, to me, they were still a "them" that was beyond me.

Little did I know that even though I would always be uniquely me, I was also completely one with all that exists. At this stage, while I could intellectually understand this concept, I wasn't yet consciously living this paradox. I was mostly identifying with my finite self, and periodically expanding beyond it into my infinite nature.

Despite my lingering doubts and fears, I relied on these Energies. Healing occurred in my clients time after time. Many physical symptoms cleared up in them as a by-product of my opening into a more expansive state of consciousness. Gaining confidence, I risked letting go even more into the increasingly potent flow. Some of my clients were quite skeptical. Their skepticism gave voice to my own doubts, which I got to practice answering with confidence. Ironically, their doubts served to strengthen my certainty that the Energies were reliable and real.

Soon people began flocking to my door because people's lives were changing rapidly. It was becoming more difficult to deny that something significant was happening. My clients' progress far exceeded anything I had achieved without the Energies. There were visible signs of people's increasing well being that I could no longer deny. They were ending stale relationships, finding fulfilling love, resolving inner conflicts, embarking on new life paths and improving their health. They were living proof that something magical was afoot.

Simultaneously, I was suffering from severe health problems, myself. While my clients were improving dramatically, I was degenerating physically. Zealous in my efforts to help as many people as possible, I worked sixteen-hour days, seven days a week. Through overwork I found myself flattened with six viruses and bottomless fatigue. By sheer force of will I continued to work through constant fevers, aches, chills, and stabbing sore throats.

So possessed was I by my mission of helping people heal and get "there," it never occurred to me to stop and see where "there" was, or if indeed there was any "there" at all. I was driven by trying to "save" people in addition to simply discovering the joys of being present with them. I was not yet able to be truly caring and present with myself and was driven to heal, fix and perfect myself.

But despite this driving ambition and its associated illness, in the process of my own awakening, many different non-ordinary senses were awakening by themselves. I began noticing how I could not only hear inner voices and feel energy, but I could see into people like an x-ray machine down to subatomic matter. Speaking of x-rays, I would feel them at the dentist's office when I had pictures taken of my teeth and I could smell and taste their energy.

As my senses opened more, I began to hear the sounds of particular organs when they were healthy or sick and taste people's emotions. This would occur when focusing on my-self as well as on others. However, shifting my own beliefs enough to understand what was causing my illnesses and dis-ease was another matter. I needed a lot of help with that.

In the midst of one of these viral bouts of chronic fatigue, a heavy, middle-aged woman came for a healing. She complained of a chronic stomach pain of unknown origins. Extensive medical tests had revealed nothing. As I scanned her energy field, I saw a large gelatinous blob of green slime in her abdomen. When I asked her if she was aware of its presence, she responded that all she could sense was the pain. She had no clue as to why it was there.

As I looked more carefully I saw that this blob had a round squat body and a recognizable face with distinct features, like a ghoulish demon. He was spewing green slime, sticking out his tongue, and threatening to grab me around the neck if I tried to dislodge him from his comfortable lair.

Resorting to a tactic I had read in a healing book, I retorted, "I'm not scared of you!" Actually, that wasn't true. I was afraid, but determined to stand my ground. He had to go. I focused a beam of energy into the woman's abdomen, surrounded the demon with light, reached my etheric hand into her body and began to pull. He resisted, re-doubling his efforts to maintain his entrenched position. Before I knew it, we were engaged in a deadly fight for which I did not have the strength in my weakened state. By sheer force of will, I managed to extract his protesting form from my client. He glared at me threateningly as I pulled him out of the woman. Jumping out of my grasp, he flattened himself against the ceiling in the far-thest corner of my healing room where he sulked and glowered at me.

With an explosion of delight the woman pro-claimed that the pain was entirely gone. She ex-claimed that this was the best she had felt in ten years. She could hardly contain her euphoria as I escorted her out of the house.

I, on the other hand, was exhausted and drained. I had been tired before this episode and was now stretched way beyond my limits. I returned to the healing room to clear the demon from my house. This involved an effort to project energy into him thereby raising his vibration and sending him into the Light. In my depleted state, this normally simple procedure was beyond my capacity.

In resignation, I left the room, closing the door tightly in a futile hope of containing him until I had more energy. Seeking to restore myself I went into the kitchen for vitamins. No sooner had I taken a swig of water in order to swallow a handful of supplements than the demon appeared. He grabbed me around the neck and choked me so hard that the pills became lodged in my throat. I couldn't draw a breath and was certain I was going to die. Gasping for air, I fell to the floor. The impact of hitting the hard tiled floor dislodged the pills. Mercifully, I could breathe once again. The demon laughed hideously and disappeared back into the healing room.

Instantly, I left the house and drove the distance to spend the night at Gabriella's house to regain some strength. I prayed he would not follow me to her home in Vermont from my home in Massachusetts. Fortunately he didn't and I spent the night in peace. The next day I asked several friends to help clear him from my house. Together, our joint energy raised the vibration sufficiently to escort him into another dimension with ease. He turned into light and disappeared.

Later that day he appeared for a brief moment in an entirely different state of being. He was luminous and gave me a very gentle, benign smile. To my utter shock, he apologized for playing out his former hideous consciousness on me, and thanked me for liberating him from it. I forgave him and smiled back. While greatly relieved, that battle left an indelible impression on me. As the gentle voice had so wisely advised before I entered this life, you don't win by fighting.

I had regarded him as an enemy I had to get rid of, instead of simply a being with its own vibration and worthy of love. Had I held him in compassion, he could have up-regulated his own energy to match that compassion and gently shifted form. I also held him as something outside of myself, rather than as my own creation and my own co-creation with my client. I wasn't aware how he was a projection of my own fight.

After this incident I redoubled my commitment to allow rather than fight, and returned to work quite humbled. This change allowed a greater flow of energy once again, and my practice became more effective. People began asking me not only for personal healing but to teach what I was practicing. They hungered for instruction in working with energy for healing, accessing spirit and understanding the principles of awakening. It seemed that no sooner had I learned something new than people were asking to learn. So I began to teach what I was discovering.

One day, I went for my usual morning walk with my beautiful Golden Retriever named Shamuki in the field across from our house. While he was romping in his inimitably joyous fashion, instead of keeping pace with him I stopped to eat an apple and to watch him. I began to notice the sun's gentle warmth on the side of my neck, as if fingers were caressing me. My senses suddenly awoke even more than usual, as if I had been completely asleep until that moment. I could truly feel at a whole new level, as if for the first time.

Like fingers, the sun's rays were pouring energy through my skin, filling each cell, enlivening my body. It was warm, every cell full of the luscious substance of life dancing. The Earth was reaching up her hands, holding my feet. I could hear the music of the universe, feel its pulsations and sense it's exquisite emotions. I was part of the very fabric of the Universe celebrating its "isness," its being-ness. I was experiencing Source in its unmanifest potential and in its ongoing process of creation.

In feeling ecstatically merged with all aspects of Nature, I experienced myself as part of an ever-changing kaleidoscope of life. The states of being I touched—through allowing, trusting and sur-rendering—far surpassed everything I had ever achieved through force of will and control. "If this is really what life is about, it's beautiful," I pro-claimed to the sun. "I choose to continue to sur-render!" I declared to all of creation. While still in this sublime, transcendent state, which continued over several hours, Shamuki and I walked home very slowly, experiencing together this magnificent connection.

In seeking further exploration of oneness, a few weeks later I took a trip to the mountains near Santa Cruz, California, overlooking the Pacific Ocean for a weeklong silent retreat. My intention was to follow my inner voice without reservation, determined that wherever it led me, I would follow. By now I was in the habit of listening inwardly for messages, but I had never attempted to listen every minute of every day for an entire week.

This degree of consistent focus was a formidable task in concentration and deep listening. All twenty of us at the retreat, though aware of each other's presence, were primarily focused inwardly. This inner world consisted of my breath, sounds, emotions, body movements, sensations, thoughts, feelings and energy.

The exquisite beauty of the natural setting supported our inner journey. We were located on a mountaintop surrounded by statuesque redwoods. Dense fog rolled in over the mountains in the early morning, only to be burned away by the sun, revealing a sparkling ocean in the distance. Inquisitive but shy deer, an ancient white horse, and a few scruffy stray dogs completed the scene.

The first day was torturous and seemed to go on forever. Gradually, as I became acclimated to attending to every nuance of my inner flow, time ceased. In this timeless place the days and nights blended into one unbroken stream of life.

One day, I awoke to the feeling of rain. The air was heavy and the sky threatening. I inquired inwardly about how to begin the day. I sensed to get up, put on sneakers with warm clothing and go out to walk on the mountain. I followed a path that beckoned and soon found myself at the foot of an extremely steep incline.

My inner voice was propelling me on at a good clip up a steep hill. I knew I was not physically capable of this task and asked to be infused with enough energy to carry me up the hill. Inhaling deeply, I began.

The incline was horrendous and after an embarrassingly short distance my thigh muscles burned, my lungs ached, and I gasped for breath. Images flashed before me of people dying on a pyre from smoke inhalation, being sent to death in a gas chamber and drowning at sea. Somehow, through all of this, I made it to the top. Exhausted, I crawled back to the large retreat room and lay down on my mat to rest. Within several minutes, my inner voice instructed me to get up and do the same climb again.

By now my breath had stabilized and my leg muscles had sufficiently relaxed, so while the thought wasn't pleasant, I didn't put up too much resistance. The second climb went much like the first except there were no flashbacks and it seemed I was building some stamina. Even though I was still gasping for air, my legs seemed to have a bit more strength as I completed this 45-minute circuit.

Once back in the lodge I collapsed again and rested. The second climb had taken more from me than I had realized. As I was drifting in a dreamy state, I could hear thunder in the background and sensed the air becoming dense. Again I heard, "Get on your sneakers. It's time to go out again."

I couldn't believe what I was hearing! I had already pushed beyond my limits twice, and now it had even begun to drizzle. The first two times I had followed the instructions without question. This time I balked. "What if it starts to rain hard? What if I get wet? What if I can't manage to complete the climb?" A firm voice responded, "Put on your sneakers. It's time to go, NOW!" Reluctantly I complied, remembering my commitment to follow my inner guidance absolutely.

Putting on a heavy sweatshirt and sneakers I set out for the third time. By now it was drizzling steadily and I hoped the heavy rain would hold off until I returned. As fate would have it, as soon as I reached the base of the steep incline, the skies opened up. Thunder crashed, escorting a torrential downpour. I was soaked to the bone within seconds.

I puffed and panted up the impossibly steep and slippery hill, feeling I would die. My sneakers grew heavier as they became waterlogged. Thick muddy clay was clinging to the sides of the shoes making each step heavier than the last. In utter exasperation I shook my fist at the heavens, "What are you guys doing to me? I'm getting really angry."

Soon there was no energy left for thought. I was forced to surrender to the movement of my body, to the rain, to the incline, to the air searing my lungs and to the burning muscles in my legs. I felt myself pulled into an altered state as if some higher force had taken control of my body and was now carrying me effortlessly up the hill.

After reaching the top, the force left me and I staggered back to my room. Stripping off the drenched clothing, I gratefully pulled on warm dry clothing. Exhausted beyond belief, I plunked down onto the edge of the hard wooden bunk bed. In utter frustration and incomprehension I demanded, "Okay guys, what's the deal?"

The response came in a wave of energy that almost knocked me over backwards, and then pushed me forward again. I was rocked back and forth. I could feel my sitz bones boring into the wooden bed frame. This rocking, which had begun with very large movements, picked up speed, becoming smoother and increasingly refined.

I began to feel a powerful hot current of intensely pleasurable fire making its way up my spine. It felt like a serpent had uncoiled in the base of my spine and was unceasingly pushing its way upward. As it did, my body began to buzz and shake involuntarily. Tears welled up and sobs emerged from somewhere deep within.

I rocked, sobbed and shook uncontrollably as this serpent of fire wound its way up my spine, burning out the debris in its path. By the time the snake reached my head the tears and shaking had subsided. They were replaced by an ecstatic flow, which enlivened every cell. My entire body was now vibrating with a new energy.

As the current pierced the top of my head I became aware of another movement beginning in the sacrum, as if two smaller snakes were waking up. This time, instead of the one current flowing up the center, there were two currents, one on each side of the center, weaving back and forth. It slowly dawned on me that these three currents were the kundalini snakes described in Indian literature.

I remembered hearing stories of people going insane from a premature kundalini release, as the energy is extremely potent. Somehow, I was in ecstasy despite my fear of being harmed. Now I understood the wisdom of pushing my body, which had seemed like madness to me. I had pushed my body beyond its resistance so that the energy could break through and open me up.

As the central current or snake and the two side snakes completed their upward journey, they stayed present, creating a smooth golden flow. As they pierced the crown of my head, wave after wave of ecstasy washed over me like an eternal waterfall. I luxuriated in these blissful energies for hours, absorbing the well-earned healing balm for my aching body as the energy rose up, spilled over and washed me clean.

CHAPTER 6

sakkara
temple of healing

Eager to discuss my recent experiences with Joffrey, I called him to find out when he would next be visiting Gabriella in Vermont. He wasn't sure, but to my delight, informed me that we could speak over the phone. This meant that I could speak with him regularly! When I spoke with him briefly, I had the sense something was about to happen, but I did not know what. He kept mentioning the highest path, warning that the highest pathway could be as wrenching and debilitating as the lowest if I were not properly prepared.

In light of all of this accelerated intensity, I sensed I was preparing for some kind of major change. But I had no idea what that was. What if I had to face more than I could handle? And what else should I do to properly prepare?

Since I couldn't imagine what would be occurring, my mind conjured up various kinds of losses: I'd be out on the street, I'd lose all of my money and be robbed of my material comforts, I'd become an ascetic with little to eat, live in a monastery and wear robes, or I would sleep on dirt floors.

Rationally, I knew that this was not what was forthcoming, but there was no end to my mind's fearful imaginings. Yet, I was also excited about unknown possibilities and potential. Something was stirring and I was eager for it to be revealed.

I had been in private practice for about fifteen years. Even though after each amazing opening the energies pouring through would be more potent, and people's awakenings would accelerate, I was eager for something new. I began to sense that this upcoming change would alter the nature of my work. There was an urgency, an immediacy about the change, so I suspected that a new form would be arriving soon.

The first whispers came when I was working with a man who had a brain tumor. He was the uncle of Isaac, the tall dark haired man with whom I was currently in a relationship. Initially, Isaac's uncle wanted me to "fix" his tumor. I explained that I could not do that. I could never predict what a person's physical, emotional or spiritual response would be to the healing. One could heal into life or death, as their own soul desired.

Isaac's uncle, reminded me of my father in several ways. They were about the same age and stature. Both possessed a kind heart but did not express their feelings easily. They both had little emotional involvement with their families. My father had kept his distance through his work, while Isaac's uncle had spent his time at the golf course and polishing his Mercedes. They were both somewhat alienated from their wives and children.

Although my father had been generous with money, his lack of demonstrable affection precluded forming a close emotional bond with him. This, I had always resented. Therefore, I was surprised when I felt compassion toward Isaac's uncle.

Mysteriously, I found no need to project the anger I felt toward my father onto him. Instead, I was empathetic to his plight. He was in a great deal of emotional as well as physical pain and was now willing to make some changes in his life. My sole concern was to help him do so.

I reminded him that it was not too late to change. Even one moment of authentic love shared with his wife and sons was worth everything. He didn't have to wait until his death was imminent to express the depth of his feelings for them. Reassured, he began to relax and open.

I realized that he would not have been able to open had I remained resentfully locked tight. He was able to yield because I did not blame him. Instead, I communicated forgiveness and understanding. As he forgave himself for his past, thus dissolving his self-judgment, I forgave my father. Isaac's uncle and I surrendered into the Love together.

As my heart filled with peaceful compassion, I became aware that a strong presence had joined us. I felt myself drawn into its embrace and consumed by its power. Suddenly it spoke aloud within me. "Shaqqara, Saqqara, Sakkara, Temple of Healing. In Thy Presence Be I Whole."

I was startled by the strength and clarity of the voice, not to mention the content. Instantly realizing that this message was not to be lost, I excused myself from Isaac's uncle to write it down. Listening to the whispers of Light again, I received an explanation. "Saqqara is the ancient Egyptian Temple of sound and healing used for the process of awakening. The "sh" is the pre-Egyptian pronunciation. You will use it as Sakkara because the "k" goes with Anamika."

"Use what?" I asked in confusion. This time there was only silence.

I was overcome by the beauty of this experience but failed to comprehend its meaning. I looked down in amazement at the words I had written: "Sakkara Temple of Healing, In Thy Presence Be I Whole." Still in a daze, I wondered what this could possibly mean. All that I could understand was that it seemed to fit the pattern of the opportunities and the highest path Joffrey had forecast. While I was quite willing to take advantage of new opportunities, I didn't comprehend what the opportunity was. Impatiently, I wanted to understand the meaning of Sakkara.

Since this wasn't possible in that moment, I reluctantly returned to Isaac's uncle. While I had been across the room writing down the message about Sakkara, he had come to the realization that he was ready for his life to change right away. He resolved to put love first, and to ask for forgiveness of his wife and sons.

He left my office in a state of peace. I later heard from Isaac that shortly after he healed with his wife and sons, he gently made his transition into death, feeling complete.

As if in answer to the need for my life to change as well, the next day I received a brochure in the mail. "Come tour Egypt, the ancient Nile and the Temple of sound and healing at Saqqara." I was amazed at the synchronicity, but now even more confused as to its meaning. I sensed the brochure was an attempt to further illuminate me, but I had no idea what some ancient Egyptian Temple had to do with my new path.

I did not go to Egypt to visit Saqqara until years later. At this point, even without knowing anything, I felt compelled to follow the clues as they presented. It was like a magical mystery tour. Sakkara was calling and I needed to follow and discover its meaning. Intuitively, it seemed vital to my new life. I was too sick to actually travel, so my next task was to investigate in a different way and find out what it was.

To embark upon this journey of discovery, I decided to give up my entire practice. Although very frightened about letting go of my clients, I began preparing them for the change. I informed them that I would no longer be available for private sessions as I was heading in a new direction that I could not yet articulate.

Not surprisingly, many people felt I was being impulsive and following a fantasy. Others warned that I was not making a sound financial decision. Some were very encouraging, while others felt abandoned. I addressed this change with each one of my sixty clients personally.

I had to agree that leaving my practice did not appear to be logical, but the feeling of Sakkara was so absolute I decided to follow this inner voice and take the risk. Taking a deep breath, I approached the edge of the proverbial cliff and jumped. I let go of my entire work life as I had known it in a period of three short weeks and opened to discovery.

After terminating with my clients, I gathered a group of twelve of my most sensitive students of energy healing to participate in my inquiry into Sakkara. As soon as we were comfortably seated in a circle, an expectant hush fell over the room. I invited Sakkara to make its presence known.

Suddenly, powerful healing energies began to rain down upon us. First, a large etheric pyramid descended into the room offering a protective container. Then a sphere appeared, representing the space-time continuum in which we live. Within the sphere was a three-dimensional star tetrahedron, the Star of David, symbolizing union with the divine and the principles, "As above, so below. As within so without."

Next, a crystalline column descended into the center of the room. Coiled within it were twelve golden strands of DNA. These strands radiated from the crystalline column and connected with each person's DNA. Following the column, a cube, a rectangle, a golden spiral and many other geometric forms appeared.

A large, rapidly spinning vortex strategically placed itself in the center of our circle. It sucked out the low frequency energies emanating from us and transmuted them into white light. The vortex accelerated or decelerated as needed. A golden column connected down through each person's crown as multicolored sheets of energy permeated the room.

Golden strands of light wrapped around the outside of the group and through each person's heart, weaving us together into one unified whole. An infinity sign appeared in the center of the room, intersecting the crystalline column. Then a multitude of infinity signs drew together giving the appearance of many gyroscopes oscillating rapidly.

After the geometric forms appeared, the door, which had been tightly latched, dramatically blew open. A powerful gust of cool wind entered the room. Standing in the center and visible to all was an etheric form of Yeshua along with angels, Ascended Masters, and Archangels. Yeshua walked around the room touching each person on the heart. I noticed each person look at him as if he were physically there. Each felt his sweet compassion and many burst into tears.

Several Ascended Masters surrounded each of us. They would circulate throughout the room approaching whoever was in need of healing. Shamuki also made the rounds, placing his paw on a heart, laying his head in a lap, or licking away tears. A powerful healer in his own right, he was accustomed to working with clients hour after hour, year after year. I had seen him perform countless beautiful and touching healings as he moved people to tears with his tender love. He participated in Sakkara too.

By now, the room was pulsing with such a charge of energy that people were experiencing spontaneous physical movement and emotional release followed by insight and revelation. By the end of this first experience of Sakkara, I knew that something extraordinary had occurred. The course of my life had irrevocably changed. I realized that Sakkara was the answer to one of my two questions, what is my purpose? Being able to invoke these stunningly powerful energies of awakening called Sakkara was to be the form of my work for the next period of time.

I was elated by my first experience of Sakkara, but had so many questions. I called Joffrey for a conversation almost immediately afterwards. I hoped he could explain the extraordinary event that had just occurred. The Chief, my friend the Native American shaman, came into Joffrey's body to address my questions. I immediately asked him for information about Sakkara.

He explained that Sakkara is a being with its own consciousness that is also one with me at some level. Its purpose is to help bring about healings and awakenings. It's an intermediary, connecting me with God/Goddess/All-That-Is. It expresses in many ways from words to extra-dimensional geometric forms of light to pure consciousness. Apparently, I was only touching the tip of the iceberg.

The Chief went on to say that Sakkara's energy is not received through any techniques or practices but through openness. It helps us experience more of our own energy directly. As it raises the vibration in the room, we naturally open into our own multi-dimensional consciousness and connectedness with All. Its purpose is both individual and planetary awakening. It helps us open again and again so that gradually we can live in our more expansive nature.

I had thought that Sakkara was simply an energy that surrounded the planet. When the Chief told me that it was a live being, I realized that it was a conscious matrix of energy. I had previously experienced pieces of Sakkara, but not the whole of it as a live being unto itself with its own consciousness.

Understanding this allowed me to relate to Sakkara in a more meaningful way. I was in an actual relationship with it, as with a lover. I became aware that Sakkara and I worked in concert in what the Ascended Masters called the Great Work. Our combined efforts were to help with the ascension or awakening of individuals and the planet.

After these revelations, I realized that Sakkara had always been with me. At each step I had been working with a version that I could handle at the time. Nevertheless, the energy that had come through me for my clients and students was, in fact, Sakkara—but now more potent than ever before.

In my childhood there had been only a small flow of its energy available. There had been no identifiable Masters, geometric forms, or intense epiphanies. The verbal messages were not as specific or articulate. As I grew and my own consciousness expanded, so did my ability to receive Sakkara in a more potent way. The Ascended Masters and Archangels came as a group energy. Therefore, I couldn't distinguish between the different beings.

I had arrived at a watershed moment in my relationship with Sakkara. My heart had opened enough that I was now able to invoke Sakkara in a fuller form, replete with its complexity, power and intricacy. Each time I invoked it, it revealed more of itself to me. We were evolving together.

I now felt more confidence to invite the energies of this exquisite being for groups of people. Previously, I had simply acted on faith that something beneficial and transformational was occurring. The more I understood and trusted Sakkara, the more magnetic and potent it became.

I began to offer the energies of Sakkara to larger and larger groups. Whether there were twelve or several hundred participants, each person was able to focus on his or her own awakening within the context of the whole gathering.

Each person's responses to the energies of Sakkara were different. Some would emit sounds, some would move, while others expressed profuse emotions or became silent and still. The common denominator was an increased awareness as all took the next step of their awakening.

I began inviting musicians to play live improvisational music using drums, flute, keyboard, saxophone, kalimba, bells and voice. The music followed the rising and falling tides of Sakkara's energies.

As I continued to present Sakkara, the transformations became more and more evident. The results were beautiful to behold. People were experiencing magnificent breakthroughs and revelations. Thankfully, my new path was unfolding more exquisitely than I ever could have imagined.

The presence of Sakkara was training me one step at a time to trust opening ever more fully into Love. Every time I offered it to others, I experienced more of the magnificent majesty of multi-dimensional consciousness. Looking back, I can see that it was like training wheels for Sakkara was playing an intermediary role between me and my direct contact with God/Goddess/All-That-Is.

My experience of Sakkara at this stage was also the same as my experience God/Goddess/All-That-Is. It seemed that it was outside of me, bigger and more powerful than I was and that I needed it. Clinging to the notion of hierarchy, I thought I needed something more special because I wasn't enough in and of myself. Since I didn't experience myself as one with All on a consistent basis, I held myself as the less important one and something bigger as the more important one. I equated size with importance and power.

While in the embrace of Sakkara, I would feel one with it entirely. I continued to believe that it was the source of my work, and that I was so lucky to have a secret weapon or magic tool I could use. I couldn't yet comprehend the paradox that while Sakkara was its own being and one with All, it was also completely part of me as well. I was me and part of Sakkara and one with All as well. We were all part of each other.

Over time I progressed from the experience of letting Sakkara's energies flow through me to experiencing them as part of my own consciousness and radiance. Eventually, as I realized I was part of everything, I could simply shift my focus from more limited to more expansive parts of me for different purposes. For example, grocery shopping versus offering groups.

These shifts in my perceptions were reflected in the change of name from Sakkara Temple of Healing to Sakkara Temple of Awakening. Eventually, I stopped using its name at all in my work. This leap of faith was frightening at first, but I came to trust that I could simply show up as me. I was enough.

soul mate

Before receiving Sakkara, I had led workshops on many topics, including healing addictions. After connecting more directly with Sakkara, my desire to offer other workshops vanished. Only Sakkara held my interest. However, there was still one 'healing of addictions workshop' that I had scheduled prior to this shift as part of a series I was presenting in Orlando, Florida. I decided to complete the commitment, as it would be the last one.

I was packing my suitcase for Orlando when Joffrey called to tell me that he was in need of a healer. He went on to say that his inner voice had suggested that he call me. I was extremely surprised, pleased and more than a bit nervous about shifting roles. I had come to rely on Joffrey's guidance, but I knew nothing about his personal life. Nor did he know anything about mine, because during our conversations he tended to have no recollection of what had transpired.

Since he was my main source of help in my awakening, what if I couldn't give him what he needed and then he wouldn't help me anymore? The stakes seemed astronomically high, but something urged me to say 'yes' so I invited him to my workshop as a guest.

The morning of the workshop I met Joffrey at the front door of the venue. While I was delighted to see him, my palms were clammy. I was quite anxious as to whether or not my skills as a healer were good enough. I felt I was going to be tested and judged by him. If I were judged negatively, I was sure I'd lose him. Fortunately, I didn't know at the time that Joffrey was extremely skeptical about healing work, for then I would have felt even more pressure to perform.

When the workshop was over, Joffrey reported that during my energy transmission he felt etheric fingers and hands all over his body poking, prodding, and rearranging him. I was relieved that he had experienced something. This gave me the confidence to audaciously offer him a private healing session right then and there. He very hesitantly agreed.

When we entered Joffrey's hotel room, I felt even more awkward than I had in the workshop. He seemed strange and distant. He plunked himself down in the large chair, folded his arms defiantly across his chest, and peered at me with suspicious skepticism. He told me that he had called me only because his inner voice was insistent that he do so. He said that he was open to traditional psychotherapy, but he wasn't so sure about this weird spiritual energy stuff I did.

I was shocked by his attitude. What did he think it was that *he* did with me? Talk about weird spiritual energy stuff! I held my tongue and took a deep breath to calm the fears rising within me. I walked over and positioned myself in front of Joffrey's chair. His extreme skepticism unnerved me. Inwardly I tensed, assuming I was in for a difficult ride because most people who came for sessions were more open.

I was panicking internally and didn't know what to do. So I closed my eyes for a moment to ask Spirit to help me handle this sticky situation. In a flash I realized I'd have to give up any agenda of helping him—or of proving myself to him. I could see I was putting too much pressure on myself by taking false responsibility for fixing him and for determining his response. I wasn't allowing him to be where he was with his own responses and reactions. With that insight, I surrendered.

Instantly, Sakkara's energies came flooding through me in such a torrent that I was almost knocked off my feet. I felt my hands being moved by the energy so I surrendered into the dance. My fear dissipated as I sensed Joffrey allowing my energy transmission into his body. He let out an audible sigh, slumped down in the chair and uncrossed his arms. I felt his spirit lift up and entwine with mine in a way that was more ecstatic and passionate than anything I had ever felt before. It felt as if we were making love, and in a more beautiful way than I had ever experienced.

Having previously done many personal and group healings, I had certainly been privy to stunning energies before. But never had I felt that I was making love with another being in this way and at this level of intensity. It seemed that all of existence was directly making love to Joffrey through me and simultaneously to me through Joffrey.

When the healing finished, I was shaken and em-barrassed. I couldn't tell this man that I barely knew that I felt as if we had just made love. How-ever, we had shared an intimate connection that could not be denied or defined in any other way. It was an unconventional twist on love at first sight and now I couldn't wait to see him again.

The next time Joffrey came back to visit Gabri-ella in Vermont, he asked me for another healing. Each time there was a potent connection between us. It was electric and magnetic. But neither of us spoke of what was occurring.

Many months later Joffrey and I compared notes. He told me that he had experienced exactly what I had. He confided that it was confusing for him when he, too, felt that we had made love. He had felt a romantic intimacy of the most profound kind, much deeper than anything he had experienced before. It had been disconcerting for him that we didn't know each other personally but were shar-ing something so intensely intimate, deeper than anything he had experienced before.

As a result of that conversation I realized that the depth of love I had experienced with Joffrey was the same feeling I had experienced with the Chief. My mind began to race. Was Joffrey in fact my real soul mate?

I was still involved with Isaac and was very fond of him, but our connection did not touch my soul the way my experiences with Joffrey did. I wanted that intensity with a partner. I wanted to be touched so deeply that doubt and uncertainty disappeared as we were transported into Love.

But strangely, despite the depth of my connection with Joffrey, on a practical level it didn't seem to me we were at all well matched. Our personalities were in such opposition that I didn't see how we could possibly get along. We would be constantly on each other's nerves because of the differences in our approaches to life.

What stunned me was that despite these differences, there was something between us so compellingly electric and magnetic that we were drawn together. I thought about Joffrey incessantly. When we spoke on the phone, I felt an explosion of consuming flames throughout my body. It was as if my whole being ignited into an expanded reality. We were one organism, united in a dance of passionate, timeless communion. Yet, it seemed odd to have this intimate connection without the usual harmonious personality ingredients present.

Not knowing what would happen between Joffrey and me was frustrating to my controlling nature. I wanted to know definitively whether or not he was my true soul mate—even though I didn't think he was. And I wanted to know now! I felt a deep, eternal bond between our souls, even though our personal journey had just begun. My image of the ideal soul mate did not resemble Joffrey at all.

Desperate for clarity about our relationship, I decided to ask him for insight. It seemed strange to ask Joffrey about Joffrey himself, because the subject was the medium. He usually didn't remember our conversations anyway because he went so far out of his body. So, I reasoned, there was no need for concern.

As usual, the Chief didn't answer my question directly. He simply indicated that we were with each other because powerful growth took place. He also advised me to stay in the moment with the situation and not try to figure it out. In ad-

dition, he informed me, the purpose of relationships is for growth.

*Staying in the present and discovering what unfolded was
certainly good counsel. It hadn't yet occurred to me to question the whole idea of soul mate that was then so culturally
popular. I had just bought the story of "The One" hook,
line and sinker since childhood. I was looking for the perfect
man to match me.*

*Although my deepest journey was about continuing to open
to more experiences of Love—like the ones with Joffrey—I
kept thinking there was something wrong with me that I
hadn't yet found "The Ideal One." I still thought that the
point of opening into infinite Love was to lead me to the
perfect man—my true soul mate.*

*I didn't comprehend that as I opened, I was drawing in the
opportunities I truly needed for even greater openings, and
that this had nothing at all to do with finding a "perfect"
soul mate or Twin Flame. It also didn't occur to me to question the notion of a single soul mate, many soul mates and
a Twin Flame, even though they were so commonly accepted
in certain communities. What if reality was really different
than we thought? What if those concepts were far too limiting? What if we made them all up?*

My mind argued that the ultimate purpose of my life was to be with the right man and to fulfill my life's mission. But some part of me knew better. While relating with others through intimate relationships of all kinds was certainly a vital part of discovering and sharing more of myself, it was not the end "purpose" of my life.

With time, I realized that in looking for the ideal man, I was unconsciously giving away my power to a mythical person and anticipating that he would be my source of love and comfort in life. Thus, I mistakenly thought it was because of Joffrey that I felt the way I did given how potent our energetic connection was.

This was a challenging perspective to shift because we are trained since childhood to look to those bigger than us as the source of our love, safety and nourishment. I thought that if I could have that special someone, I would feel the way I wanted to feel. It seemed reasonable to want to be with another person so it took a while for me to recognize that the way I was actually envisioning a love relationship with a man was from an attitude of need fulfillment, entitlement, possession and consumption.

This stemmed from the fact that I was approaching life from a perspective of being separate from the source of All. Despite all my direct experiences of Love and my growing awareness of oneness with All, I still perceived myself to be in starvation, lack, and survival when I wasn't in an exalted state. So, I still believed that my needs could only be met from the outside and that it was up to me to figure out how to get them met.

It was really challenging to face how needy and demanding I was being in the name of love. Trying to fill the perceived hole was a lifelong habit, and I was only just now becoming ready to experience who I was beyond that narrow perspective. I could see that it was time to take the pressure of my demands off the notion of "The One" and focus, instead, on experiencing my oneness with all of existence.

I was ready to learn how to open into my own internal resonances of Love—consistently and by choice. From that state of conscious being, I knew I could create the kind of sharing with others that I wished for. And by experiencing myself as the very Love that I was seeking, I could then experience a more satisfying love with others. I was determined to learn how to stand in that Love no matter what else was going on in my life.

This was a major shift in perspective from the lens through which I had been looking. I had enjoyed many beautiful relationships and by all cultural standards could say that I had been "in love" many times. Yet, something inside me was now asking that I transcend all of my notions of falling in love to discover something more.

As part of this shift, I had to give up the cultural ideal of "The One" since it was far too limited for what I was yearning to experience. This took an ever-increasing awareness of the moments when I was unconsciously operating from that pattern. I saw how I was constantly scouting and searching for what was already innate.

The spiritual experiences I was having at this stage involved opening beyond my individuated little self to connect with multi-dimensional reality. Again and again, I got to leap the bounds of "me" to include infinite dimensions of existence and extraordinary beings both in and out of physical form.

So, I began a daily practice of shifting from the perspective of separation to connectedness. I did this simply by being aware of whether I was constricted in separation, or truly feeling the light openness of connectedness. I was learning to expand beyond a dualistic either/or perspective. Duality said I was either only little me, or I was connected and could lose myself in the infinite. My experiences were teaching me both/AND in which I was still me AND simultaneously one with All.

This paradox of AND beyond either/or was something my mind couldn't comprehend. But I could feel it. The experience of AND created an entirely different reality in which my multi-dimensional experiences, as well as my little finite self, were part of the whole of who I was.

When I opened beyond only the little me, I would have thrilling experiences of the love affair inherent in interconnectedness. I was opening up to more of all that existed. Each time I felt those beautiful resonances, they would be almost immediately reflected in outer experiences.

For instance, in the midst of all of this I went for a walk through a field with Shamuki, yearning for a deeper romance with the Divine. Suddenly, I felt a beam pierce my heart. It seemed to come from a spirit I had not yet met. I stopped abruptly and saw a handsome, well-shaped pair of male hands reach through the ethers. The hands were not quite physically there, but were almost palpable.

I reached to take his hands. As I did, I felt his spirit body merge with my physical body. It was as strong and real as if he were there physically. It was a beautiful experience that lifted me out of my relentlessly questioning mind and put me into the embrace of the great Love once again. I let go into it for the next few hours.

I basked in the warmth of the expansive energy of my budding romance with all of Creation. I could feel how my devotion to this union—and the sincerity of my yearning—had opened the door in my heart more fully. I was developing a new level of intimacy which was with myself and All.

For the moment I could let go of my need to know who my soul mate was, as if it were one person rather than a way of relating. Now, I basked in that warmth and let everything just be. Joffrey's face flashed before my eyes. Joffrey was on his journey, too, and whatever unfolded from here, we were in it together heading in the same direction, Home.

CHAPTER 8

white gold

I began to hear stories about various avatars such as Sai Baba, Ammachi, and Mother Meera. People I knew were flocking to see them, recommending that I go too. Friends filled me with stories about their lives. Hearing their names again and again seemed to be a message to go see them. With each passing day it became more difficult to ignore the call.

Sai Baba began showing up in dreams and visions. I would feel an exchange of energy with him as he called me to come to him. I wanted to heed this call, but unfortunately, I was too sick to make the long journey to India.

I did mange to see Ammachi since she tours the world every year to give her blessings to the millions who come to receive her embrace. Her compassion was phenomenal as she hugged and blessed person after person. Then I went to Germany to see Mother Meera. She sat on her throne in silence. One by one people would sit at her feet for a few moments to receive her energy, which was pure, clean and transformative.

I was impressed by the energy transmissions of all three. They were wonderfully healing. Still, these visits left me confused in two ways. First, despite the extraordinary grace and power that I had both witnessed and felt, I wanted to know what the lives of these avatars were like. They seemed so remote as people. They revealed little or nothing of their personalities. It was as if their personal experiences were of no importance. Their whole presence was presented through their purpose.

I wanted to know how someone with a potent energy transmission lived. Did they have lovers? Did they live alone? Did they sleep or meditate much? What did they eat? Did they take nutritional supplements? Did they have aches, pains and illness? Did they feel happy when they were not working? Did they feel lonely or empty? What did they yearn for—if anything? I had all of these questions and more.

This lack of information reinforced my false notion that an avatar is not human. It appeared to me that they had, in effect, traded their worldly sensibilities and interests for spiritual ones. It also seemed to me that this trade off was mandatory—to become more spiritual one must become less human.

I thought that to be successful spiritually it would be necessary to abstract my essence from the day-to-day life that had always defined and vitalized me while I committed to a higher ideal. I imagined that the cost on a personal level would be total and absolute.

I had hoped that Ammachi and Mother Meera would show that it was not true. I hoped for them to demonstrate that to ascend spiritually I would not have to become more perfect and less myself. Since possessing a personality and enjoying life on Earth seemed a detriment to spiritual ascendancy, if these beliefs were true, I was quite spiritually deficient. I delighted far too much in all of my friends, Shamuki, Isaac, my family, my home and all of the rest of my warm comforts.

I was not yet able to distinguish being attached to something or someone versus just enjoying it. I created an either/or, meaning I'm either attached or I renounce it. Neither was appealing.

I believed that spirituality entailed ascetic renunciation rath-er than the delicious inclusivity of all parts of ourselves. It was only much later that I learned the joy of inclusivity that came from AND rather than either/or.

These experiences with the avatars also left me confused because their energy transmissions did not feel more powerful to me than Sakkara. If I could invoke Sakkara, I reasoned, did that mean I was just like them? This was hard to believe. I couldn't see myself being anything at all like Ammachi and Mother Meera. They seemed the epitome of selfless devotion. Compared to them I felt like a normal person. I was quite perplexed by the seeming contradiction of Sakkara coming through me instead of someone like them. How could such a profoundly awakening energy come through someone who wasn't a spiritual leader serving the masses?

When I returned home from each visit to the ava-tars, I felt like a failure. I couldn't say that I had had what I would deem a life-changing experi-ence. I was just as deeply moved in the energies of Sakkara, if not more so, as they addressed me personally. I blamed myself for this. These ava-tars supposedly had extraordinary healing powers.

"Why wasn't I blown away by them as so many others were?" I asked berating myself.

I did much soul searching until I finally came to realize that while surrendering to a guru, or being a guru, is a valid path, it was not my path on either side of that coin. My own imperatives were not calling me in the direction of being a follower or leader. I was here as a pioneer, for my own awakening, and to pass that on to others in whatever ways I wished. I was not here to forsake my own personal self and devote myself exclusively to "serving" the masses, but to walk an integrated path in the world.

I noticed one other positive result from visiting the avatars. Seeing them in action, comfortable with and trusting their own transmission of energy increased my trust of Sakkara. Instinctively I knew that Sakkara was a source of great good, but every time I offered its energy, I was plagued with doubts. Will the energy come through this time? Will people benefit from the experience? Will the energies be strong enough, good enough, wise enough, loving enough? Is the energy vibration high enough?

Due to these thoughts, when I presented Sakkara, I thought I was marching to my death. I was sure that this time I would indeed discover that I was a complete failure. Why did I even bother to exist?

It wasn't that I was suicidal, but in the depth of that self-judgment, I didn't want to live. This perspective of doubt gripped me causing terrible anxiety and cutting me off from access to my own life force and self-acceptance.

I knew that my own self-doubts were not the only possible reality, but they were strong. In addition to believing them about myself, I was projecting these doubts about myself onto Sakkara. I was never good enough, far enough along, wise or perfect enough. I believed that spirituality was perfection rather than a compassionate embrace of every bit of me.

I was buying into the notion that some people are beyond human, and better than others. I was still holding a false hierarchy in place, just as I was judging some parts of me as better or worse than other parts. Determined to rid myself of these doubts to achieve some state of perfection, I pushed hard against them, punishing myself severely through doubt, disdain and criticism.

I later discovered that including every part of myself with understanding—including the voice of doubt—was necessary. Integrating all of me, from the smaller limited parts to the larger expansive parts was what brought joy. I came to see that all of the wheels in an old-fashioned watch are valuable and necessary to the functioning of the whole. As I learned to bathe myself in the healing balm of self-love, much healing occurred, and those things that didn't heal just no longer presented a problem. They could be on my proverbial bus without driving it.

Seeking clarity, I called Joffrey in hopes that one of the guides could explain to me who I was and how to be both spiritual and human. This time, the voice that came through to address me was Miriam, the mother of Yeshua, known to the world as Mary. She epitomized gentle compassion.

My burning questions were, "What is an avatar? Is it possible to become an avatar or do you have to be born that way? What if I am unworthy and the gift of Sakkara leaves me? What if that were to happen and I could never fulfill my destiny?"

She explained that while avatars are born with the gift of a transmission of energy, that doesn't mean they are perfect. They still have a lot of growth to do to mature in their own consciousness.

I was elated by Miriam's response because it basically gave me permission to be myself, and not some image of perfection. I thought about my purpose and how I wanted to carry it out. Having a powerful transmission of energy as a gift did not mean becoming a guru or having millions of people sit at my feet the way others did. It meant connecting more deeply with my inner light and letting it shine. It meant claiming this infinite nature and accepting my ordinary humanity commingled with my expansiveness; one did not contradict the other. It meant growing even more compassionate and full of love for all of me and thus everyone else.

I had mixed motivations in asking these questions. One motivation was to understand more about my gift of Sakkara and how it worked in my life, because I knew I had been born with a gift of consciousness to transmit to others. When I was an infant, my mother's sister used to come sit with me because she experienced some kind of peace in my presence. I myself could sense a state of being of a different frequency than ordinary reality within me. It was this part of me that

I adored the most and it took years to come to love the more ordinary "human" parts.

My secret motivation under these questions was a desire to end my self-doubt by proving that I was just as special as the Indian saints whose blessings I had experienced. My insecurity reasoned that if the transmission of Sakkara is as good and powerful as that of the avatars, then maybe I'm just as good.

I thought that avatars were perfect "God beings" and were more special than everyone else. I held a hierarchy of importance. I didn't yet realize they were regular humans who were learning their own lessons too and could even derail and fall off their paths.

Through my experience with the avatars I came to see that the accepted world version of spirituality was just a set of beliefs and not "the truth." I knew that if I couldn't be myself but had to play some "spiritual" role, I wasn't interested. I wanted to be real. I wanted to cherish the tiny and ordinary details of human life as well as the extraordinary. I wanted to keep discovering more of me, whatever that was. Gradually, finding compassion for every bit of myself, including my darkness, became my liberator.

However, during this period of time I was seeking to be especially good instead of flawed. Thinking that I was either were opposite sides of the same coin. Later I learned to put the 'better than/less than' coin down, but at the time this was my prison. It stopped the grace that was the natural flow of being. Then I spent my time trying to defend myself and prove my worth. I didn't understand that I was fighting with myself because I had created the belief of 'not good enough' and then spent my time trying to compensate for the lack of compassion towards myself. I eventually learned to live beyond both ends of the false hierarchy of relative value.

The kind of service to others I thought was spiritual was really self-sacrifice on the one hand and playing savior on the other. This was all I could see of others and what I assumed they too, were doing. I thought that to be spiritual we had to reject our humanity and go further into some rarified state. In the name of spirituality I was rejecting my humanity, pushing away from my body, and trying to rise higher to be more perfect.

I discovered that becoming more real occurred through deeper acceptance of all parts of me, including my human nature, which I had judged as "less than." I kept striving to find my "greatest" self. I didn't realize that this motivation came from the "little self" itself!

I gradually learned to come down to Earth and open into my own body and then far beyond, which was a process of integrating rather than rejecting my humanity. I learned to be at peace with the paradox of both/AND, meaning that I was uniquely, humanly me AND interconnected with all. I was learning that by getting to know and integrating all of me with compassion, from the smallest to the biggest, from the lightest to the darkest, I'd experience the Love I incessantly sought. I was learning to truly listen to all of parts of me and then choose which to follow without condemning the other voices.

Offering Sakkara helped with this, because every time I transmitted its energies for others, I moved beyond my doubts into a stunning experience of my infinite nature. I knew that the transmission I was born with was a gift to offer others. But I didn't yet understand that it was really a gift through which I could experience myself, since it was my own radiance of Love.

I wasn't "channeling" something that was beyond me, I was simply opening to identify with the part of me that was already there and infinite.

Once I opened into my own higher nature, its energy radiated out effortlessly, and the words with which I expressed that consciousness when I addressed the people who attended the gatherings poured out effortlessly. Thus, offering my gift called Sakkara was my own practice in accessing my own infinite nature. It also assisted other people to access their own gifts, and grow from cultivating and sharing them.

My mind spun as this new perspective began to supplant the old: You mean we're all here for our own growth and born with a gift? Our gifts are actually for us? While offering our gift can really be a blessing to others, it's the vehicle through which we get to have our most intimate connection with ourselves? I also didn't realize that the gift I was born with was a part of me and could therefore never leave. How could I lose a part of myself? I could block its expression by denying its existence or value—but I could never be separate from it. Sakkara couldn't abandon me. It is who I am at an expansive level of my being.

Instantly, I began to see visions of gold everywhere. When I closed my eyes I would see a soft white gold light. When I was working with individuals, I would feel gold surrounding us. During Sakkara, a golden mist showered the room. When I looked at Shamuki, whose fur was golden, he would be bathed in golden light. When I closed my eyes to sleep, a golden wave ushered in my dreams. I began to think that I was seeing visions of my true home. Perhaps I had come from a gold planet?

When I asked Joffrey about it one of the guides laughingly informed me that I was not from a gold planet, but from the golden ray. He explained that a ray is a powerful stream of energy emanating from Source. Intrigued but ignorant, I asked for an explanation about what he meant by the golden ray. He explained that the golden ray is the ninth ray, a high frequency vibration. In fact, it is the highest possible for humans until Dec. 21, 2012. He said that a high frequency ray was not better than rays of other colors. They are all uniquely beautiful. View the rays, he instructed, as notes on a scale, high or low in frequency. I wanted to know what color the God ray would be. He said that it was comprised of all the colors and was therefore colorless. Wondering how I could reach the God ray, I was told that if I embraced all of the rays fully they would open into the colorless ray.

I fervently wanted to achieve this, but wasn't sure exactly how. He patiently explained that there was nothing I needed to do to get there. In our natural state, we are all in the God ray. It is only our perception that we are not there that keeps us from recognizing it. This was a revelation to me; all souls are in the God ray, yet we have sent pieces of our consciousness into different densities to learn certain things. Thus, all we need to do is wake up to the truth that we are already there! There was nothing to achieve?

Joffrey's words confirmed the understanding I was beginning to internalize. He further said that we have sent pieces of our consciousness into different densities to learn certain things. Thus, all we need to do is wake up to the truth that we are already there! There was nothing to achieve.

Achievement at that time meant something to do and somewhere I needed to go. Thus, I had been fervently trying to do something to get "there." Intellectually, I understood that we are already "there," which is really "here" but I was now learning to go beyond pushing, controlling and driving to achieve something. As I dropped the constant pressure and anxiety and tension born of trying to force an outcome, I began experiencing resonant states of being which effortlessly and powerfully animated and inspired my doing.

When Joffrey reminded me I was already 'There'— and what I was looking for was available now—I became aware of how much tension I had in my body from relentless striving. I decided to let go and relax into now, as if what I sought were already available. It was as simple as gently slipping into a warm bath and letting myself relax into its all-embracing support. As I did, I was flooded with sensations of the Love I had been trying to achieve. It was always there and always available.

Prior to these revelations I had been living as if there was some hierarchy or stages I had to work through like climbing the corporate ladder—or a stairway to heaven. With this new awareness, it felt like a shell cracked off and I began to merge with a greater aspect of myself. Total bliss does not even begin to describe the sensation. I wish I could say that this state of being stayed with me, but at the time, I slipped in and out of it.

Each time I slipped back into it, I began to have more and more visions of white gold and an impulse to perform some sort of ceremony to solidify my feelings of Oneness. In one of these visions I saw a white gold ring with seven diamonds. I approached a jeweler to have the ring made, insisting that it be ready by October 13th, my fortieth birthday.

The ceremony to further connect with All began to take shape in my mind. My intention was to increase my trust and commitment, as if I were marrying God. My connection with what felt like God had increased to the extent that now I was eager to pledge myself in union to this Source of existence.

God was not yet completely personal for me and was still not integrated with my sense of myself. I imagined myself as a child of some universal power stronger and more loving than I, like when people use the phrase "a child of God."

Joffrey called unexpectedly on October 12th, his voice full of mystery. He announced that he would be flying to Boston the next day for my birthday. He hung up without any further explanation.

On the day of my birthday I awoke with a feeling of great anticipation. My first priority was to rush to the jewelers. I waited expectantly as he brought out the box containing the ring. My design turned out beautifully: three white gold rings nestled together perfectly to comprise one large ring. There were seven little diamonds asymmetrically placed around one large mine-cut diamond in the middle, symbolizing oneness. It shone magically in the light. With a high heart, I snapped the box shut, not to be reopened again until later that night in the union ceremony. On the way home, I impulsively bought six white roses for the occasion.

As the evening neared, Joffrey arrived. When I opened the door, he was standing there with six white roses in one hand and a ring box in the other. My mouth dropped open as I virtually yanked him into the house, insisting that he open his ring box. There, nestled in the blue velvet was a white gold ring with many diamonds. He told me that he had been impelled to buy this ring for himself for some kind of ceremony to symbolize his union with God. A comparison of the numerous impulses and visions we had received leading up to this synchronous event clued us into the fact that something was definitely up. It was clear that we had both been inspired to do this ceremony; and though neither of us had the slightest idea what would come of it, we were both committed.

Later that evening, a few special friends arrived to witness our ceremony. Each was given a white rose. Joffrey and I both affirmed that our ceremony was a symbolic union of our intention to know Source intimately. Sensing that other unseen presences wished to add to the ceremony, Joffrey closed his eyes and effortlessly slipped into trance. This time, no special prayers were required.

Miriam's voice spoke through him and addressed the small group gathered. She spoke of exactly what I had been wishing for, which was how to forge a more direct relationship with God.

I was seeking a new understanding of God as something real for me. I wanted to experience what it was rather than think of it as a title, or as the name of a grand being. I had come from a background of disbelief in God and I wasn't seeking faith or belief in God. I wanted to grow beyond the stage of belief or disbelief in an external authority. I was tired of begging, pleading and manipulating some imagined power to help me. If there was a living vibratory consciousness that many called God, I wanted direct personal contact with it.

As energy from Sakkara and unseen presences flooded the room, I let myself melt into and entwine with this sublime lover. Dissolved into the fullness of my heart, I could suddenly sense the presence of God directly. There was a distinct difference between this experience and that of Archangel Mikael, for example. I sat in the sacredness of the moment as we all sat in silence looking at each other while gazing inwardly. I had committed to the union with my own inner divine Source and there it was.

There was a long pause and the energy shifted ever so slightly. Joffrey's voice, which had sounded like a woman filled with compassion, transformed to a man's voice with a strong resemblance to Miriam. Instantly I recognized her son, Yeshua. He spoke of his own passion for God in his heart that was born of his absolute devotion, rather than stringent practices. He stressed that devotion was a choice one made again and again, not once and for all. His voice was full of emotion as he shared the beauty of his own passionate devotion.

I was relieved to hear that only devotion was needed because I had never been interested in any practice other than moment-by-moment self-awareness. I was growing beyond my perceived separation, one step at a time. Luckily, I had no idea of the persistence of old beliefs I would get to face and untangle.

I was amidst a life-changing process. What I had considered reality was falling apart. While I had some sense that this was occurring, I couldn't truly understand intellectually the magnitude of what was underway in my life. But like Yeshua had described, what did help was my absolute devotion to viscerally knowing myself as Love more intimately. I could feel the earnest yearning and passionate calling of my own heart for greater union. I felt compelled to bring that forth again and again. In fact, this devotion became so strong and unwavering, it almost felt like an obsession. Yet it was born of my desire to more intimately commune with creation itself. This passion consumed me night and day.

Joffrey gently opened his eyes. While not remembering the exact words, he too felt the presence of God in his heart and in the room. We were held in the sacredness of the moment as we sat in silence looking at each other. We had both further committed to the union with our own inner Source in a beautiful and sacred sharing. And those who joined us for this ceremony joined us in that deepening experience.

Without speaking a word, we both reached for the boxes that held our rings. Joffrey ceremoniously placed my ring on the ring finger of my left hand. I did the same for him. In so doing, we were not only symbolically wed to the divine, but were pledged to each other as soul mates for eternity, companions on our journey into greater oneness.

CHAPTER 9

the doorway

The idea of a more personal, intimate relationship with God was thrilling and I was eager for it to happen. I imagined it to be like talking to another person with whom I was in love but much more intense. In this process Joffrey and my unseen friends had much to teach me and I had much to learn. My imaginings, no matter how seemingly beautiful, got swept away. I was like an athlete training for my first marathon and they were my coaches.

In my communions with my unseen friends, I would expand into my greater self. I would touch into realms of beauty that were indescribable, and I wanted more. I wanted to live there permanently and to experience my own existence as a state of being of Love. I knew that awakening was real and it was happening. By the same token, I didn't feel the way I thought I should. I wasn't sure what an awakened state felt like, but I knew it wasn't how I felt at that exact moment.

I had been introspective and focused on self-awareness since I was a small child. Taking that further, at age nineteen, I became involved in a peer counseling movement. This was an organization in which every participant was both a counselor and a client. The recommendation was that each person give and receive one session per week. I would regularly give and receive six. That's how fervent I was about awakening. I had kept up that pace for fifteen years and as such had been able to clear out quite a bit of internal baggage.

After all of this, I was perplexed and infuriated that I had still not "arrived." While I touched into the great Love I craved more and more often, I was still unable to consistently access it as a permanent state of being. I still had not been able to fulfill my dreams of life partnership and a powerful unfolding of life purpose. It seemed that the task was not only daunting but impossible.

I kept thinking there should be an end to the process, even though intellectually I knew there wasn't. I was pushing hard, trying to hurry up and get somewhere so as to be finished. Finished was an image of perfection, which meant arriving at a point of permanence that never changed. I was threatened by the continual loss of control in the ongoing processes of integrating and enlightening. I wanted them to stop rather than going on forever.

I was plagued by the belief that I had a fatal flaw I had to fix. No matter how much Love I experienced in any moment, it was never good enough. Something was always wrong. I believed it was I who was fundamentally wrong. During the moments I opened into Love as a state of being, I was at peace. Then after that, I would enter the old belief again of not being good enough.

This journey is easier said than done, I thought. Somehow it seemed that I had spent more time in life with my imagined badness than in the beauty. Each time I came up to this doorway, I became aware of the depth of fear that still resided in me, despite my desire to go through it. I didn't know what it was about, but I knew that there was some deep darkness lurking in crevices into which I could fall if I wasn't careful. I recoiled from this horrifying abyss for I felt that it could destroy me.

At this stage, I was trying to eliminate 'my badness,' not simply illuminate the belief *that I was bad. I couldn't yet accept that the part of me that believed in my badness might always be there as part of our human hardwiring. When I relinquished trying to eliminate it, I was able to focus on giving and receiving love. In the state of Love, I expanded beyond judgment and was at peace once again.*

It was years before I was able to accept the existence of this hardwired belief without blaming myself for its presence or trying to rid myself of it. Eventually, I found compassion for the part of me that held this belief, and was able to take it into my own heart with tender kindness. Through acceptance, I could let it be there without believing its negative propaganda about me or following its suggestions. This allowed a lightness and freedom beyond the persistent sense of being fatally flawed.

During this period, choosing to love was an important focus that brought me through the doorway into peace and freedom each time I remembered to make that choice. I was progressing a little at a time.

Simultaneously, I began to sense the possibility of opening into other dimensions that were very light and beautiful. It seemed I was way up on the mountain and if I could get through the doorway all would be full of wonder. However, if I didn't, it was a long way down. In an instant I could be in heaven or hell.

It seemed to me at that time that there was something I could do right to gain a reward and feel wonderful, or do wrong and feel terrible. I didn't yet know that the mountain was made of my own beliefs. I wasn't yet able to see so much of what I called "reality" as simply the reality of my own beliefs, not something objective and carved in stone.

I began to understand that the healing work I was doing with others and myself was raising my vibration. I was resonating with higher and higher frequencies, gaining greater and greater access to a multi-dimensional reality. The more I acknowledged and accepted my fears and the underlying assumptions that created and fueled them, the more my experiences of Love deepened. I could sense I wasn't just some empty receptacle for Spirit to fill, or the proverbial hollow flute. I was vibrating that state of being, experiencing ever-expanding consciousness as an embodied state that was real and in which I lived.

Despite this palpable progress, at times I felt quite inept. I still did not have my soul mate or the fullness of my mission. No matter how hard I tried, no matter how many lessons I learned, my two primary dreams remained unmet. I couldn't cope with this and wanted to speed things up.

Whenever I would go into pain, it was because I was frustrated that my ability to control my life wasn't working. I was rejecting the present moment, as it was, demanding it be the way I thought it should be.

I was judging the darkness as bad and the light as good. As such, I wanted to avoid the dark and head for the light. This judgment was keeping me from experiencing everything as it was in each moment, which caused suffering.

Trying to control life came from a childhood belief that I had to do something to get my needs met. I remember wanting love from my parents and at times it wasn't forthcoming. I found many different strategies to try to manipulate someone to give it to me. As a child, I wasn't yet able to find it within myself, or get it from someone else, so I was always seeking it or pushing away from it, pretending I didn't need it. I became fiercely independent, pretending I didn't care. "I won't ever get close enough to anyone to let myself be hurt again. I'm just FINE and I'll handle it myself, so there!" Unbeknownst to me, this child part of me was still running the show.

As an adult, I was learning that if I allowed myself to be present, I would experience the truth, which is that the presence of love and safety were already within me as palpable states of being. If I slowed down enough and became suf-

ficiently quiet within, I could tangibly feel their resonance vibrating within me and all around. Then, as an expression of those resonant states of being, outer physical demonstrations would precipitate into form almost instantly.

Still, despite many sublime experiences and demonstrations that this is how reality works, I continued to believe that I had to do something or get someone to meet my needs. Shifting from being outwardly focused to feeling how my own inner resonances met my own emotional needs was a very new way of being, a change in paradigm.

Each time I went there, it was frightening to let go of control. But when I accepted my fear of the unknown and opened into these fulfilling inner states of being, outer manifestations would appear in the most surprisingly wonderful ways. I was growing toward consciously being able to choose to feel my inner resonances—and allow for their joyous and miraculous outer expressions—even during times when the negative self-perception arose.

I was discovering how effortless and elegant life really could be. For example, one night I went to bed thinking that in the morning I really HAD to trim my rose bushes. When I woke up in the morning, they were all trimmed, and so neatly that I was astonished on both counts! I didn't have a gardener, and no friends or neighbors could have snuck over the fence in the middle of the night to accomplish this task.

The next day, to compliment the beauty of the roses, I was considering hiring a gardener to clean the leaves off the front steps and walkway. Minutes after this desire crossed my mind, a gardener, whom I had never met, walked into the yard with his leaf blower and cleaned off the steps and walkway. This took only a few minutes and he left as quietly as he had entered.

Weeks later when I chanced upon this man at my neighbor's house, I thanked him profusely, offering to pay him for his services. He declined saying it was a gift. When I asked him why, he stated quite simply, "Because I knew you would appreciate it."

At each new step of surrendering control and opening up, I encountered fear. When loss of control became overwhelming I called Joffrey to get some perspective. As Joffrey accessed our unseen friends, I felt the presence of an ancient philosopher join us. While his words of wisdom regarding the perception that something was missing in my life certainly rang true, I felt no better.

As I was complaining to him that despite his words of wisdom I still felt fear, suddenly, I saw a hand holding a bright blue sword coming toward me. I gasped. The philosopher informed me that it was the signature of Archangel Mikael. He instructed me to place my hand over Mikael's as he cut away my fear. I did as he instructed and instantly felt much lighter.

Then I complained again. "The fear is lifting. But, I still feel empty. I wish something could infuse me and fill the emptiness which has replaced the fear."

This time he instructed me to let Mikael come into total union with me. I didn't know exactly what he meant, but I relaxed my body and allowed Mikael's exquisite energy to help me.

The philosopher continued to coach me to allow Mikael to fully embrace me in an intimate and even sexual way so that we could totally merge. I was embarrassed and shocked by this suggestion, but found myself consenting.

As the philosopher was speaking I suddenly felt Mikael filling me with his presence. The energy became so sexual that I felt as if he were making

142

love with me. His maleness far surpassed anything I had ever before experienced, and in the throws of such energetic ecstasy, I suddenly remembered that the philosopher was present. I flushed in shame and embarrassment about being observed in such an intimate state.

However, the union with Mikael was so potent that I couldn't resist, so I let go more. I realized that I had focused on a man as a soul mate because I had known nothing else. Here I was experiencing an intimate connection and union in a way I never could have imagined. I realized that I was not alone, that the dimensions interpenetrated each other. I could engage in dialogue and interaction with beings from other realms, like Mikael. We occupied the same space at the same time, simply dwelling in a different frequency band.

I closed my eyes and took a deep breath, allowing myself to be filled with the love I felt with Mikael and all of the different beings I had encountered multi-dimensionally. Mikael's energy filled the emptiness and opened my heart. Gentle peace descended and my pain lifted.

"How can I hold this," I queried nervously?

"You don't need to. That would be more control. Just be present and attune to it now," came his patiently loving response.

With those instructions, I let go entirely into Mikael. Joffrey stayed on the phone with me for a few more minutes. When we hung up, I was floating in Mikael's embrace and could feel him still with me. As it was evening and soon time for sleep, I didn't even bother taking off my clothing because I didn't want to move. I stayed right there on the bed infused with his embrace until the sun rose the next morning.

CHAPTER 10

obsessed

After many more similar encounters with Mikael and other beings, I became even more obsessed with enlightenment. I could do nothing but sit still for four, five and six hours at a time as energies rushed through me. Not only was the lusciousness captivating, but I was driven by a fierce determination to obtain enlightenment—still believing it was an ultimate state that could be attained and retained once and for all.

I was drawn to go inside of myself so strongly, I could pay attention to nothing else. Previously, the only time I sat still for this long was with my clients. In my work, I had been engaged in a single-pointed focus for eight to twelve hours a day, allowing energies to move within and through me. Sitting still now had a different quality. There were so many sensations rushing through my body I was compelled to be with this process to the exclusion of other activities. Drawn by the Light that guided me, I plunged deeper and deeper into the darkness of the Mystery. I cried from the exquisite beauty, and from fear of the unknown.

I had habitually avoided the unknown, fearing it as a place of darkness that could destroy me. My mind wanted to know everything ahead of time, as if that would keep me safe. I was about to discover that the unknown is alive, sentient and full of unlimited possibility. I came to find that I could gently slip below the surface of what was known and feel not only truly safe but also alive with exciting potential discovery. In entering the unknown, I got to know more of me. As I began to relate with the unknown in a more trusting way, I engaged with it in a beautiful, rewarding dance that was my soul's call to adventure.

Rushes of energy consumed me, coursing through my body like torrential rivers. I felt grabbed, as if strong hands held me in an invisible vice and I couldn't move. Sometimes those hands would rock me back and forth moving me around like a baby. I had no control over my movements and would often end up flat on the floor. I was forced to surrender to something far greater than my little self.

I had yearned for this greater power to consume me and draw me into its embrace. It conveyed such a sure strength that I felt safe to let go in ecstatic abandon. As I surrendered, this powerful force tenderly but insistently penetrated to my very core. I felt touched to the depths of my being.

Whatever this was knew everything about me and held no judgment. I had no secrets and was utterly naked with nothing hidden or withheld. This was the Love I had yearned for my whole life. I wanted nothing more than to be where I was, totally surrendering into its cradling and penetrating embrace.

Was this enlightenment? I didn't know. Whatever it was, I was in ecstasy, and wanted more and more. So I persisted.

Yet, as these energies continued day after day, hour after hour, I began to feel irritable and tense. The intensity kept building, but with no release. I desperately sought relief. I was going wild, about to scream or jump out of my skin if something didn't break through. At my wit's end, I called Joffrey for help.

"Things are moving so quickly," I began. "I thank you for your assistance with that, but I request even further acceleration so I can get this over with."

It was the same wise philosopher whose voice addressed me. His calm inquiry into what results I was seeking only infuriated and inflamed me even further.

"Total enlightenment immediately. I am about to jump out of my skin! Since our last conversation I've experienced profound energies and a lot more love. My frustration is that there is something I can't quite move through yet. What do I need to do to pierce through into complete enlightenment?"

I was frustrated and hated feeling this way. I resented the sheer magnitude of the process, not to mention the difficulty of the task. It seemed never to end; there was always more. I had no gratitude for the process and wanted it over NOW.

His calm voice came back with an inquiry into what I meant by enlightenment. Again, this frustrated me even more.

I was in the trap of thinking there was something to attain and somewhere to go that was called 'Enlightenment.' Even though my consciousness was steadily expanding into new realms, I was still striving to attain my idea of enlightenment—which was some static state of bliss. What I really needed was to revel in gratitude and to trust the ongoing process of 'enlightening' and integrating.

There was a natural back and forth movement inherent in this process that I was experiencing. And I had to learn to go beyond the mistaken judgment that said that some days I was going forwards and other days backwards. That wasn't true, no matter how it seemed. I was simply unfolding and experiencing different parts of myself, sometimes repeatedly but more deeply each time.

I began to become aware that thoughts about time, instead of trust in right timing, pulled me out of the moment. When I wanted things to go faster or slower, I left the moment. When I thought I needed to make something happen in a certain amount of time or by a certain date, that pressure took me out of the optimal flow of the moment. When I flowed with the moment, everything occurred easily in right timing.

Finally I became aware that the source of my suffering was that nothing was the way I thought it should be. I constantly wanted my life to be different than it was, and I wanted it RIGHT NOW. This demand was causing my angst.

Finally, the philosopher began to assuage my frustration by drawing a distinction between skills in using energy and real awakening. He explained that many people had mastered skills in the use of energy for all kinds of positive and negative purposes, but that it wasn't the same as ascendant awareness. The latter was being truly at peace with all of who you are in each moment. Then in each moment through this deep acceptance, one lives in one's infinite nature beyond the perception of time. In this timeless state of being, all feelings and challenges are welcomed as an opportunity to go deeper into that infinite nature.

Then not surprisingly, because the philosopher loved to teach by telling stories of other Masters, he began to tell me of the Buddha's dilemma. Like me, the Buddha had tried to perfect himself, but it never helped him feel the way he wanted to. He was still in pain and frustration.

When he realized there was no more he could do, he wanted to die. I could relate to that, having felt that way many times. So he sat beneath the infamous tree to do just that. But paradoxically, he had already mastered so many energy skills that instead of dying he had a huge realization that although he thought he had a fatal flaw, he was actually a good and beautiful being just as he was. Sitting under that tree, he felt the truth of this so profoundly in his heart that he suddenly found freedom from the pain that had been tormenting him.

When he went to tell others of his realization, they wanted the practices he had done to get there, even though he explained that it wasn't necessary. So Buddhism was born of those practices.

Hearing the philosopher's version of the Buddha's dilemma helped me realize that I was not defective after all. I had felt stupid because it was taking me so long to grasp what the great Masters seemed to achieve so easily. It was reassuring to know that even they had all struggled with the process.

He reassured me that each time I entered into the moment, it would be as if I were always there and as if the old paradigm of control had never existed. He recommended that I just do it for that moment and not try to do it for forever.

When I relaxed into the moment and let go of my demands that anything be different, I could feel the great Love again. That wonderful state of being was so different than the paradigm in which we had all been raised that I sometimes I thought I was losing my mind. Blessedly, in a good way

I actually was losing my conditioned way of thinking—as has every pioneer, visionary and genius in every field who steps far enough outside of consensual reality to access inspiring innovation.

Finally, despite my fears and concerns, I recommitted to what I adored the most. I surrendered yet again into the delicious, luminous Love that was the essence of all of creation.

CHAPTER 11

strange occurrences

I continued to be absorbed in marathon sittings. On New Year's Eve, I was slowly coming out of one of these long sessions, preparing to drive to Isaac's house, when suddenly I felt something inside of me crack. My body softened, as if it were melting and dissolving.

Although it was an unusual sensation, I was not the least bit afraid as I found myself swimming in a sensuous sea of love. As I became part of that amorous liquid, I became so spacious and languid that the boundaries of my body seemed to lose definition. I couldn't tell where I stopped and where the air around me began. It was like bathing in waters of ecstasy, which were both within and all around. It was better than floating in warm amniotic fluid.

In this state, I could barely walk much less drive. I got in the car anyway and drove at 15 mph down a 65 mph four lane highway to Isaac's house. When

Isaac saw me he was concerned, but not overly so. This wasn't the first time he had seen me in some non-ordinary state of consciousness.

"I don't know exactly what's happening, but it feels incredible and I know it's good," I reassured him. My words were to reassure myself as well. Most reassuring, however, was being held in the warmth and safety of his generous arms. I was dissolving and I didn't know how far it would go. I thought that perhaps my body would dissipate entirely and I'd be released into Spirit.

Throughout the night and into New Year's Day, this delicious dissolution continued. It held the promise that I would be released into something special and wonderful. The sensations were so extreme that I couldn't talk, move, or interact with the world. Despite fleeting thoughts that I might be going crazy, I had a very deep sense of the rightness of what was happening. It was what I had imagined enlightenment would feel like; so I was able to let go into it. I could do nothing else anyway, as the process was in charge. I was not.

After melting for sixteen hours, I began to feel as if a ceiling were opening above my head as something inside of me opened. The energies intensified to a fevered pitch and my body began to rock wildly. A terror of annihilation rose up in me until I found myself screaming, "I want to go home! I give myself, my whole being over to you. I surrender!"

Suddenly, I felt as if someone reached down, grabbed me and pulled me up through the dimensions. A beam of energy pierced my chest and went directly into the heart of my heart, the inner sanctum. A beautiful circle surrounded by tiny diamonds—just like my ring—was placed in my heart to symbolize a union, a coming home. I found myself face to face with a presence, as if I could reach out and touch the face of God. Gratitude welled up inside of me and a torrent of tears streamed from my eyes as I honored my connection with All.

In that moment of blissful surrender I felt memory after memory, identity after identity falling away. I heard myself shout aloud, "I'm free! It's happening!" A group of Ascended Masters came rushing toward me. Among them were The Chief, Gautama Buddha, Yeshua, Merlin, Miriam, and Isis. They nodded their heads, honoring this event. It was a most glorious reunion and celebration as I realized that these were my best friends; I had always been with them.

My mind began to race, "Am I enlightened now?" I heard a gentle voice reminding me that there is no enlightenment, rather an infinite process of integrating and enlightening.

Still unable to move, I stayed in the energies. Gradually the waves flowing through my body slowed down to such a degree that I was released into a state of pure consciousness. At one point, I opened my eyes and looked down toward my legs. My entire physical body seemed to have disappeared and was imperceptible to my eyes. All I could see was black.

I couldn't move from this void state for five hours. Gradually, I felt some tingling around my mouth as the tissue began to revive. It was like warming up out of a deep freeze. I was slowly able to emit some inarticulate sounds and eventually a few words. Then my head began to rock, generating an impulse that moved down my spine and enlivened my extremities. Finally, I was able to stand and to gingerly walk again. I felt like a toddler taking my very first steps.

Isaac was his usual kind and concerned self. He held me gently in his arms and stayed close through the night, bringing me water to drink. While he himself was not experiencing what I was, he was tender as he could see the vulnerability and intensity of what going on. His eyes were warm and his arms secure.

It was soon after this experience that strange and seemingly magical things began to occur. The first one happened when I attempted to reproduce my body in my imagination and send this body double to Gabriella's house. I wanted to see if I could project enough energy to audibly ring her doorbell. Seconds after I imagined this, the phone rang. It was Gabriella. She frantically told me that she had just walked out of her house to get in her car, and her car was gone.

"Gabriella, exactly where was the car parked? Was it near the doorbell?"

"Yes, it was parked where I always park it, directly in front of the door. Why?" she demanded.

"I have a funny feeling that..." Gabriella interrupted with a loud yell, "Oh, my gosh, there it is way over in the bushes!" She dropped the phone with a sharp clang and ran out to examine her car. I stayed on the line waiting. She returned breathlessly, "My car is in the bushes lodged between two trees, but so neatly placed that there's not a scratch. How on Earth did it get over there?"

"Could it have rolled?" I asked.

"No, the ground is perfectly flat," she replied. "When I pulled in last night, I put on the emergency brake and locked the doors as usual."

"Is there a strong wind, or could someone have pushed it?" I persisted.

"Anamika, what is going on?" she demanded suspiciously.

"Well, Gabriella," I began hesitantly, "The only thing I can think of is that I attempted to ring your doorbell and I missed. Sorry."

It was difficult to believe that the energy I had sent had been strong enough to move a car, but there was no other explanation that seemed plausible.

In my attempt to create a facsimile of myself, evidently my energy hit the car instead of the doorbell with enough force to move it. It appeared that my innocent little experiment had moved her car as a mechanical response to energy.

The second odd thing occurred during a workshop I was leading in Northern California. It was a thrilling experience because Joffrey had joined me while I was transmitting Sakkara's energies. It was such a magnificent marriage of energies—Sakkara and the wise perspectives that he brought—that Joffrey and I felt this must truly be the work we were born to do together.

The entities who spoke through Joffrey were able to explain the function and purpose of the energies as I was transmitting them, thus adding a wealth of understanding. As I was recounting the story about moving Gabriella's car, just as I got to the part about ringing the doorbell, an actual doorbell began to ring. Stunned, I stopped my story and Joffrey jumped up and ran to the door to inspect. Since we were in a hotel conference room there were no doorbells to be found. Clearly, the sound had come from the ethers.

Several minutes later, the lights first began to flicker and then blink on and off in an odd, irregular pattern. We called the hotel staff to report the problem. They informed us that there was no difficulty with the lights in any other part of the building.

Then, as if this wasn't already a strain on my credulity, Joffrey and I went to the house he was temporarily renting during the lunch break. While he was in the living room gathering some materials for the afternoon, I walked toward the kitchen to prepare lunch. As I rounded the corner into the kitchen there was a huge crash, clatter and bang. I jumped and let out a startled shriek.

Joffrey came rushing in to track down the sound. As there was nothing visible, he began to open the cabinets. We found that all of the pots and pans in the cabinet directly across from where I had been standing had come crashing down off their shelves. They were lying in a disorganized heap on the cabinet floor.

After lunch, when I checked with Joffrey about the various phenomena, the guides explained that the doorbell ringing and the lights flickering were orchestrated by them and that the dishes clattering was another mechanical response to my energy. They went on to explain that the reason there appears to be structure to the physical universe is because energy moves so extremely rapidly.

After hearing their explanation, I thought the issue of phenomena was complete. However, I was proven wrong when my favorite black wool sweater mysteriously disappeared. I had taken it with me one evening in case the temperature dropped. It was casually draped over my arm as I was engaged in conversation with Isaac. While we were speaking, I had noticed it on my arm and one second later it was gone!

Isaac and I immediately sprang into action to find the sweater, dashing up and down a steep flight of stairs several times in vain. We questioned everyone in the vicinity as to its whereabouts and came up empty-handed.

Prior to this series of energy events I would have been certain that I had mysteriously lost the sweater. However, now it appeared to have dematerialized in this dimension and shifted into another. More than likely there is a spirit running around who is quite warmly and elegantly dressed!

I greatly wanted to understand more about the process of enlightening. Do phenomena always occur? How does life change? What does one become? I had so many unanswered questions.

It was fascinating to hear of the lives of the Masters from Spirit's perspective. They spoke to me at length of extraterrestrial involvement on Earth with humanity and told me stories of how Miriam got pregnant and gave birth to Yeshua, contrary to popular myth. It was not an immaculate conception, nor did he die on the cross they explained. They spoke of many well-known human events, such as the parting of the Red Sea from a perspective of ET technology and not as some mystical occurrence. What they shared seemed more plausible than what had been passed down as historical truth.

They were trying to show me that I was not alone in my experiences and in fact, was following in their tracks. They wanted me to understand that Ascended Masters were ordinary humans just like me. While this was reassuring, with all this awakening, why was my personal life in such a state of unrest? First, there was my relationship with Isaac. We had a very sweet emotional connection, mutual respect, and comfort. Yet I did not feel passionate love for him. Our relationship felt more like brother and sister, so my urge for deep emotional intimacy was not satisfied.

Isaac insisted that if we got married, we could grow into that deep love with each other. He argued that relationship is a spiritual path and if I made the choice to commit, the passion would grow.

While he had a valid point, I didn't feel that I could marry him on potential. I also didn't feel that any amount of work would take us to the passion I longed for in relationship. Yet, with Isaac I felt safe, and I didn't want to let that go.

I was still having visions and dreams about a tall man with dark hair and blue eyes. I could not let that image go. I had to find out if I was crazy or if this man really existed. He felt like the one with whom I wanted to be. I had a very clear picture of this man, down to the brand of shoes he wore. In fact, every psychic I'd ever consulted described the same exact picture. Didn't that prove he was real? Maybe it was my mind's projection that others read in my energy field. I didn't know. All I could say for certain is that his image persisted; it would not go away.

I couldn't understand how I could feel him so strongly, as if he were so close, and yet he never materialized in the flesh. It was becoming more and more agonizing not to be with him, nor to know if he even existed beyond my own imagination.

Joffrey hinted that his image was my mind's projection of some idealized man and that people were reading that in my field. Even though I trusted him, I couldn't let the image go. Unable to solve this dilemma, I threw my energy into my work life. I held several groups a week, which were profoundly fulfilling. At the same time, Joffrey and I were getting closer. Whenever we spent time together our connection would instigate tremendous growth for both of us.

When we simply touched each other anywhere, currents of energy would open up in each of us and long buried emotions would surface. Because Joffrey was very frightened of confronting issues directly we couldn't directly discuss what arose. This was far beyond frustrating for me. I have a photo of myself as a baby with a pink plastic telephone receiver in one hand. That moment—captured on film—accurately forecast my love for verbal communication and the thousands of hours of sessions I gave people by phone!

Even though Joffrey would discuss nothing with me personally, after our conversations, he had some awareness that something had changed for him even though he could not specifically say what.

Joffrey and I were yin and yang about everything, even about our unseen friends. I couldn't get enough of them and he couldn't resist them strongly enough. He couldn't believe that I was so open and I couldn't believe that he was so closed.

Spirit would talk to Joffrey and advise him what would be of most benefit to him and he'd do the exact opposite. In addition, the most spectacular healings were still continuing to happen when he would let me work on him and when he would consult his inner guidance. I lived for those moments and he couldn't wait to get away from all of it. We were continually in a tug of war.

Despite this, Joffrey felt compelled to spend time together. Our souls were woven together by some invisible thread and we had shared our divine wedding ceremony. Even though we constantly encountered problems inter-personally, I couldn't keep away from him. This was confounding. What was also confounding was that as I was receiving so much love from Joffrey, Sakkara and Shamuki, I was beginning to experience more and more self-hatred.

Much darkness still lurked beneath the smooth surface. I was the image of composure. If every single detail of life didn't go the way I expected, I would blame myself and conclude that I must be a terrible person. My expectation was that life should be seamlessly smooth and graceful, without any challenges. Needless to say, it never was.

Therefore, I thought that life wasn't working because there was some horrendous flaw in me. I was too ugly, too fat, too controlling, too manipulative, too ungrateful, too something or not enough something else. I'd find some reason to beat myself up because nothing ever measured up to my image of perfection. This meant that everything was my fault for which I needed to be punished.

I faced example after example of how brutally un-forgiving I had been toward myself. This harshness was miles from gentle self-acceptance and self-love. Fortunately, I understood that recognizing these patterns was a vital part of the process. I was becoming more proficient at noticing the mechanism at work. When I would catch myself going over my list of personal failings, I would stop, admit that I was doing it, take a deep breath and forgive myself for engaging in self-blame again. Then, I would recall and open to feeling my inherent goodness.

Each time I reconnected with the Love inside of me, my connection with it grew stronger and the bouts of doubt and self-hatred diminished. Little by little I was softening into self-acceptance. Since this state of being felt so much better than self-punishment, I vowed to remember to take a breath and connect with Love each time I caught myself walking down the road to an internal hell. I could see that I was progressing though it felt like only a little at a time.

the theft

My appointment book disappeared! One moment it was with me, and the next moment it was gone. I was in my parked car and had taken it out to check an address. I know for certain that I put it back in my handbag when I finished. Less than five seconds later, I reached into my bag to take it out again to find a phone number and it was gone! I took some momentary solace in the fact that I never lose anything, so I looked again. It wasn't there. I searched my bag and the car ten times over. No book!

My heart was pounding, and I was desperately trying to calm down. It's only an appointment book and I never lose things, I lamely reassured myself. However, an hysterical voice in my head reminded me of the numerous times I had told myself that if I ever lost my book, my life would be over. So much for calming down—I was moving into a full-blown panic attack! "Where is my book? What am I going to do? It couldn't have just disappeared and I couldn't have lost it; I'm too organized for that! Where is my book?"

Then, I remembered that if I really calmed down, I might be able to hear an answer to that question. I took several deep breaths and waited. An unnervingly steady voice seemed to indicate that it had taken my book. "What do you mean you have my book? You mean you dematerialized it like my black sweater? Is that you speaking to me, God?"

"Yes, Anamika, I have your book."

I seemed to recognize this straightforward voice immediately as God, but it could have been any of the spirit pranksters I had been meeting. I called Joffrey in a panic for a conversation to see what was going on. "I'm going to talk to you through Joffrey about this tomorrow!" I threatened.

"Very well," came an unruffled reply.

I was framing this situation as if God had taken the book. At this time I didn't have any concept of our power to simply enter a different reality in which the book wasn't there, so I said that God had done it to me.

Later, I could see that we create our reality constantly, but mostly without any conscious awareness of doing so. And since I was expanding my consciousness through my passionate explorations of higher frequencies of energy—and the unusual phenomena this would precipitate—I would sometimes experience what some have called an inter-dimensional overlap.

I would have experiences of being in one place and then moments later being elsewhere, with no memory of having traversed the distance. I see now that I was simply creating myself in a new space with no awareness of doing so.

The next day Miriam came through Joffrey to speak with me. She told me that it was important that I surrender the book entirely and trust God to give me everything I need. She said that it was time to let go of the part of me that was highly organized and linear because I often carried that to an extreme to try to make myself feel safe. She told me that the loss was actually an opportunity to let go of that fearful part of myself. While I understood, I wasn't happy about it to say the least.

Here was a chance to trust in the goodness of God. I wanted my book back, but I also wanted to do the "right" thing. I wanted to do what was best in God's eyes. I was terrified of doing the wrong thing and consequently became confused. I didn't know whether to try to get my old book back or to go out and buy another one.

"What should I do?" I asked Miriam. "How do I know what is the highest path? Should I just go out and buy a new book or just wait to see what happens? I can wait a few days but, I do need to know where I am supposed to be and at what time. Eventually I'll have to have something to write in."

In my panicky state I became aware of being like a little child who was trying so hard to earn approval from some big parent in the sky. I was trying to do what I thought I "should" do—otherwise there would be disastrous consequences from this power that was larger than I was. I was so scared of being judged and punished for getting it wrong that I burst into tears.

Miriam's voice addressed me again, inquiring as to whether I wanted to speak with God directly.

"Speak to God? Well, uh, yes, I would," I gasped in shock.

The voice of God began to speak through Joffrey in a direct, matter-of-fact way. Unlike the Ascended Masters who had uniquely colorful inflections, God sounded almost like Joffrey's usual speaking voice.

As soon as I heard God say my name, I burst into tears. I couldn't believe it! I was talking to God! I could feel the immensity of God's intense and direct love. It was absolutely overpowering. Wave after wave of love washed over and through me. Cascades of bliss and rapture rendered me helpless and entranced. All I wanted was to be swallowed alive and never come out. I wanted to stay in this palpable state forever.

It was the most astounding contrast; the absolutely prosaic voice of Joffrey combined with the presence of God. This love overshadowed the immense and pure love I had felt from the Chief, Yeshua and the others. I had come to associate Joffrey's slight vocal alterations as an aspect of the presence of other dimensions. It was hard to accept that God needed nothing but pure love to communicate. Joffrey's voice would do just fine.

By now, I was shaking from fright. Racked with conflicting emotions, I was torn apart by the magnitude of what I was feeling. I wanted to embrace God through Joffrey and at the same time grovel in adoration. I wanted to leap into "His" arms and share all of my secrets, knowing that I was safe from all harm. Yet, I feared that I would be judged deficient and relegated to eternal obscurity. Somehow, I had to prove myself worthy of God's love. The only solution was that I be torn apart belief by belief and remade anew in a better form.

God let me know that the purpose of this encounter in this form was to help me further our union by learning to be with him in more ways than before. God paused, then wanted to know what questions I would like to ask.

The extreme contrast between my panicky, self-judgmental state and the warm, unconditional presence of Love was never more evident. This experience was by far the most immense and pure Love I had ever felt. It was hard to accept that communing with God needed nothing more special than sharing how I really felt.

Even while in this Love, I was wracking my brains to see what was really important to ask or say because I still wanted to do it 'right.' My first impulse was to ask about my appointment book, but I quickly censored that thought. As much as it worried me, I couldn't very well qualify that as important.

I realized that there wasn't anything at all practical that was important at that moment. Nothing mattered but the feeling of God's Love. Yet I had so many questions. I dropped down beneath my mind into my heart to what I deemed a real question. Still afraid of being wrong, I tentatively ventured, "God, how can I love you more?" The message that came back was that I couldn't love more than I was doing.

The Love radiating from God was so exquisitely compelling that I felt helplessly drawn in. I didn't want it ever to end. This was the Great Love I had been seeking, the one that touched my innermost yearning. This Love was not only everything that I thought I would experience with the ideal soul mate—it was much, much more.

Bathed in this much Love, my fear stood out in stark relief. Everything was exposed. I was embarrassed and ashamed of myself, a far cry from accepting. Still, I was beginning to feel bolder, so I asked for more. "God, I have so much fear and judgment. Can you help me with this?"

I could sense God communicating that he accepted me completely, even with all of the fear and judgment I was exposing. I sensed that the disappearance of my book was to help me find freedom from these fears. Strangely enough, it was beginning to be pleasing that this had happened. I had a glimpse of the freedom that would be available if my attachment to the book could be broken. This possibility was light and liberating and I felt like laughing. I also felt an unexpected pleasure that I wasn't in control. For someone who thrived on being in control, I was surprised by the abundant joy of such surrender. What a relief! I didn't have to micro-manage my life! There was a higher presence that was wiser than the controlling part.

Even though I knew better intellectually, I still was acting as if this higher presence was something other than me that could reward or punish me; so I was in the habit of trying hard to control my life to get it right. Yet, each time I opened to commune with something larger than my little controlling part, it was a powerful step toward greater peace and freedom. I was in the process of learning to reference my heart's desires rather than forcing and figuring things out in my head.

Finally, I admitted, "I can see that by always trying to do the right thing, I truly don't know what I really want." I was utterly afraid of doing things wrong. Making mistakes was a form of death in my mind. I attempted to focus on what I would ask for if I weren't afraid of being imperfect. Nothing came. I was stumped if being imperfect was okay. With nothing to lose, I asked the question that I had thought was too imperfect to ask, "Can you tell me why you took the book?"

The response that came back stunned me. I repeated back what I heard with a question: "It's because of your desire to be closer to me? My focus on getting everything right was in the way of us connecting more closely?" This was absolutely the last motivation I would have imagined and the antithesis of what I had assumed. I could not have been amidst a more glaring example of how little I knew of God from my limited perspective. I had thought I was being punished. Yet, actually, through my appointment book—which I thought I would die without—I had built a testament to my fear and ignorance and it had been taken away from me.

God's desire for our closeness thrilled me no end! I felt myself sigh from the relief of understanding the great book robbery. God's desire for closeness and mine were the same. I offered back, "I don't want anything to come between us either. I can feel that you are loving me, beyond my own judgment. I am also feeling confused right now, and speechless."

Since I had an image of who God was and none of what was happening fit that image, my world was turned on its head. I had been certain that reality was the way that it seemed. Now suddenly it all seemed different. Little did I know that the way I was experiencing God at that time would also radically change again, just as the way I experienced myself would turn inside out. But that's for later.

The more Love I felt, the more the fear of judgment arose. "Right now I feel a deep fear of being judged, though I know you are helping me with this. I also feel that if I don't do it right you will take your Love away. I fear that you are going to leave before I ever really find you."

It felt so good to be able to admit these deep fears. It was as if a great stone was being lifted off of me. I now felt weightless by comparison. My breath seemed to become energized and light as I spoke of these dark concerns that I had withheld even from myself.

The presence of God reassured me that the Love could never go away. I was further reassured that God had neither the desire nor the power to do that because the very essence of God is Love.

"I'm afraid that I am unworthy of you. I don't feel that who I am is good enough."

It felt good to give voice to this fear, too. I thought I had to be someone other than myself to be fully loved. Again, the reassurance came back that I was loved fully and eternally, no matter what I was doing, just for who I am. This Love was absolutely unequivocal.

"I ache for a more direct relationship with you." I admitted.

I felt the same response in return. God aching? Now I was shocked and thrilled even more. I didn't know God had such feelings. I had no idea that God's feelings were the same as mine! I knew that I had been aching all of my life! Had God been aching throughout all of eternity? If so, I wanted to ease God's ache, but I didn't know how.

God was saying I needed to believe in myself. My lack of self-worth was not humility, but rather self-judgment. That judgment had kept me feeling separate from the Love and in great pain. Real humility was my openness to God's love and the acceptance of our union. I had always felt so alone and self-sufficient so it was difficult to admit that I needed and wanted God's love, even though I had been striving after it for years.

The pride I had taken in my fierce independence continually reinforced the illusion of separation, thereby thwarting my experience of union. This illusion had created more and more suffering. Addictively, I perpetually reached outside of myself for something to ease the pain, something like a long-awaited soul mate. I had diminished the value of the wonderful men with whom I was in relationships, and was always searching for something "more."

By now I was overwhelmed with love. "I love you with all of my heart and soul." I could feel God loving me back entirely for my body, mind, spirit, and soul—all parts of me. It was so utterly and directly personal. I had to admit that I was squirming from the discomfort that this level of personal intimacy produced, even though I so desired it.

As I surrendered more deeply into the Love, I was also beginning to fear loss because the intensity of the experience was fading. As God departed in that form, I felt myself reaching to hold on. I didn't want God to leave. I instantly felt a desperate longing to be together again in that way.

Then, suddenly the Love came back again in a torrent. I quickly realized it was still God teaching me that even though the form changes, the Love never leaves. It was I who would leave it. I could separate from it believing it wasn't still there—or bring forth my love and devotion to reconnect.

Instead of indulging the fear of loss, I decided to try reconnecting. My hesitancy disappeared. All I wanted to do was to open up every cell and fiber of my being in ecstatic mergence. I wanted to join permanently with this profound and ultimate Love that was available to me by holding back nothing. I had never before felt this degree of un-

conditional desire. Every part of me was screaming, "Yes, now!"

Taking a deep breath, I began to pour my heart
out to God. Big round tears welled up and spilled
down my cheeks. God felt my Love and responded
by pouring into me, filling me up. By now I was
crying from profound gratitude and blessed Love.

Then this energy disappeared suddenly. While
I was startled by the abrupt departure, I did not
feel the loss and sadness that I had earlier when I
thought God had left. This time I felt filled, whole,
and indescribably wonderful.

I decided I could let go of the book and when I
got a new one, I would not recreate the old one. I
would buy something smaller and lighter in which
I would record only what I needed in the present
and nothing from the past. It seemed fitting that
the new book would reflect my new awareness and
perspective. Breaking the attachment to the old
left me free as never before.

Later that day, Joffrey called sounding very upbeat
and chipper. When I asked him why he sounded
so cheery he said that he was finally getting or-

ganized. He had gone out earlier in the day and bought an appointment book so he could keep track of everything. Before I could get a word in, he started raving about what an impressive book he'd gotten; it had so many sections, it was such a nice color, and it was so well organized. It turned out to be the exact same brand, color, and style of book as the one that had been taken from me! "You have my exact book!" I exclaimed.

The lesson showed up here with graphic clarity. I needed to be freer, spontaneous, and less rigidly organized. Joffrey needed to learn focus and organization. It made perfect sense that he now had the book.

I laughed at the cosmic irony of it and the clever, subtle way that life works. The experiences for me, and for Joffrey, were both precisely tailored to what we each most needed. I had given up something I thought I'd die without and, not only had I lived, I felt better than ever! I had given up some of my overly rigid order for freedom. Joffrey gave up some of his unhealthy chaos for healthy order. I breathed a sigh of relief. How easy it turned out to be. We were both finding a new balance. How gloriously wonderful it was!

If I had known then that this was only the beginning of what I'd have to give up… but I didn't know that then. Blissfully, I thought I had done my giving up and letting go.

I had more work to do to untangle the roots of the part of me that was unconsciously trying to make another person God. I was beginning to see that as long as my primary relationship was between myself and God, the rest of my life would fall into place. I could include other people as parts of God but I couldn't look to a relationship or one person to be the whole of All.

I also wanted to accept myself beyond all considerations. Then I could welcome others into my life without the pressure of them needing to be everything on the one hand, or else judging our relationships as meaningless on the other hand. I had my work cut out for me. To traverse this challenge, I needed to focus more on knowing God as my primary relationship.

I didn't understand that through this focus, I was really focusing on knowing and loving myself as well.

CHAPTER 13

raising my vibration

I had fallen head over heels in love with God. Our conversations were the most satisfying moments of my life. I wanted every second to be as these. At the same time my relationship with Joffrey had strengthened and he more frequently joined me in Sakkara. During one such event in Sarasota, Florida, our friends in spirit discussed the process of ascension and awakening.

They talked about how we are infinite beings expressing in the finite for the joy of it. Awakened beings can hold themselves as both and are so completely in acceptance of their humanity that they remain undisturbed and non-judgmental in the face of it. The blessing of coming upon that oh so human part of us was an opportunity to go deeper into our connection with All.

Again and again they reiterated that I was in the ascension process. Even though I knew that was true I also had doubt because I still had an image of ascension as an unchanging state of bliss and light. This certainly wasn't the case with me. While I did experience otherworldly energies and other parts of myself beyond the ordinary quite often, I was continually cycling through emotional highs and lows in a very human fashion. I was always questioning why I wasn't feeling constant rapture. I had thought that ascension meant vibrating at a higher state of consciousness and embodying a different reality, one of constant joy.

They explained that the ascension process was a change of frequency and one came to live in a state of acceptance. It was awakening to the experience that we are one with the very essence of creation, which is Love.

When I was with my friends in spirit or experienced myself as one with All, I felt whole, joyous and expansive. I did not feel this way in my every day life. They understood me and what I was experiencing and I so desperately needed someone to understand. Though I had many human friends, only my unseen friends in spirit could truly touch me where it mattered. When I was not with them I felt inconsolably alone.

I thought that was how it would be forever. I didn't know I was at a stage of development in which I would connect, have an exquisite experience, and then just as quickly settle back to disconnectedness by default. Each time I touched the old program again was a signal that I was at the doorway of a greater opening. I was learning to trust that every bit of this back and forth was not really back and forth. It was more like simultaneous ascending and descending spirals, both of which were a vital part of the process.

I was learning that every person, no matter how developed in any arena, has highs and lows. No one stays in a peak experience at all times. I couldn't have imagined the lightness and freedom awaiting me born of gratitude for every tiny movement of all of it.

As I was preparing to leave Sarasota after a very illuminating Sakkara focused on the journey of awakening, I had a vision of a little beach cottage. It was dazzling white stucco set on a crystalline white sand beach surrounded by an orchard of fruit trees and tropical flowers. I felt a tingling through my whole body, and knew this was where I would live. The vision was so clear, I didn't even question that I would be leaving behind the life it took me twenty years to build. I was ready to take on a greater challenge and some new steps forward.

Later, on the plane, I was in a deep introspective state with my eyes closed when I felt the presence of someone before me. I looked up and there was Yeshua gazing at me intently. It struck me like a thunderbolt: Yeshua is my Master Teacher!

Yeshua smiled warmly. You are being prepared to connect with God more intimately. "Are you ready?" I excitedly nodded yes. "Very well then, tomorrow is the day." He bent over and kissed me tenderly on the forehead and then on the lips. I glanced down at my new, much smaller calendar, which happened to be open in my lap. In small print it said "Ascension Day"—which I later learned occurs each year 39 days after Easter Sunday.

Even though I had no idea what this day meant at the time, Yeshua indicated that it's about a window of opportunity for further raising one's vibration because millions of people all over the world focus their attention on ascension on this day, even though most misunderstand what it really means.

I awoke on Ascension Day with a great sense of anticipation because I would be leading a Sakkara later and hoped another profound connection would occur. A group of twenty people was gathered for the Sakkara. I noticed a special electricity in the air. As I breathed deeply and allowed the energy transmission to begin to move, I saw a large etheric window opening in the center of the room.

Others had noticed the window as well, and we all moved into the opening together. Each person began to experience his or her own version of the ascension process. In the sacred silence, I heard God speak to me inside of my being. "Are you ready to embrace more of your ascendant nature?"

"Yes, I am," I responded excitedly.

As the room flooded with Love, I heard: "I have always been here loving you. I never left. You chose to perceive yourself as separate to explore aspects of your being. That was a powerful choice at the time, but humanity has been cycling in that loop for a long time. You have been crying out for Love from a place of deep agony for many years. I have been here in the faces and voices of all of those around you and available directly, yet you have not seen or heard me. I have received your rage and your anguish as well as your love. It has been you who hasn't been receiving me."

The truth of this perspective struck me like a lightening bolt and I again realized that God wanted my love, too. I was overcome with the need to apologize for pushing away, and then rejecting and blaming God for rejecting me. I vowed to remember that and to consider God's point of view.

In a flash I saw at a deeper level how my yearning for a soul mate was really a desire for union with All. I had been looking for a person to fill the hole instead of opening to my relationship with the Creator on a personal, intimate level. I heard in my own inner voice:

"I am in your every day life in the most ordinary and mundane ways, which is why I speak to you in your own voice. You are an aspect of me, so be yourself completely. Trust that you are worthy. Do you question my worth? Then how can you question your worth? You come to know me by coming to know who you are. You are Love itself, the very fabric of existence."

Suddenly, a shell of my identity as I had known myself cracked and fell off. I soared through ecstasy, bliss, peace, and freedom, and was elevated into an eternal embrace. Then BOOM, I was thrust right back into my body. A veil of perceived separation had dissolved.

What seemed like God's voice spoke again. "Welcome home, Anamika."

I was stunned by the utter simplicity yet profundity of these words. I felt a crystalline clarity as if I were truly in the present moment for the first time in my life. There was no empty hole. Everything was contained in the here and now. I had no sense of past or future, here or there, inside or outside, up or down, back or front. It was all the same, all right here, right now. I laughed at this cosmic joke that I had worked for thousands of years to get to where I had been all along, right here, right now. In fact, there was nowhere to go. I realized that ascension was awakening to the truth that already existed. I could feel that the very cells of my being were Love incarnate.

I looked back over the many stages it took to get to this place. There had been poignancy, sacredness, yearning, endless hours of devotion, pleas, prayers, tears, rage, fears, surrender, and faith. When all was said and done, this moment was almost anti-climactic, so matter of fact, yet so profound. The drama I had anticipated would accompany this moment was also a misconception about the true nature of life.

"Oh, life is just life," I laughed aloud, "and I am who I am."

CHAPTER 14

imperfections

My vision of moving to Florida was quickly becoming a reality and I couldn't help feeling unsettled. Although I knew that this move was the best step for me, it was an enormous decision. I would be leaving behind my whole life as I had known it.

One of the things I would be leaving behind was my relationship with Isaac. I had mixed feelings about this. For some time now Isaac and I had been moving in different directions. I was drawn deeper on my path. I wanted to discover more about myself. I knew that I was becoming less of this world as I was responding to the dictates of my own evolution.

Isaac was becoming more and more involved exclusively in earthly things like movies and restaurants. These were of no interest to me. Yet, as much as I felt ready to end the relationship, I also enjoyed being with him. There was a certain comfort and safety that was not easy to relinquish.

At the same time that I was pulling away from Isaac, Joffrey and I were increasingly magnetized to each other. I was able to feel Love so intensely in his presence as he could in mine. Needless to say, being able to feel this deeply with him certainly got my attention and we craved spending time with each other.

I spoke to Joffrey about all of this. Just like me, he was both excited and frightened by the prospect of us becoming closer. As I lived in Massachusetts and he lived in Washington state, we spent most of our time talking on the phone. On a whim, we decided to take a trip to Mexico together. Joffrey flew to Boston for the preparation.

Excited about our upcoming adventure, we stopped at a local stationery store to buy a map of Mexico after I picked him up at the airport. I waited in the car while Joffrey jumped out in search of the map. When he came back to the car he told me that he had been unable to find a map. We were about to leave empty-handed when Merlin jumped into his body, went back into the store, found the map, paid for it using Joffrey's money, and then popped back out of his body. I was getting used to this by now. "Thanks, Merlin," I said aloud into the air.

I had been with Joffrey when different energies were moving in and out of him for so long that by now I could tell which of the Masters was present. They all had their own distinctive energy, facial expressions, verbal cadence, and accent. This presence was unmistakably Merlin.

When we arrived back at my house, Joffrey and I were sitting at the kitchen table drinking tea and pouring over the map when Merlin again decided it was time for a visit and popped back into Joffrey's body. I was able to continue my discussion with Merlin through Joffrey without missing a beat.

Merlin and I were deep in conversation about Mexico when a realtor and her clients showed up at the kitchen door. My house was now for sale as I was preparing to leave for Florida. I looked at Merlin and asked telepathically, "I hope you're leaving, right? I ask because I know that you're a prankster and don't always behave appropriately. So, I don't trust you not to make trouble." He gave me a knowing wink, so I swallowed hard, praying that this outlandish situation wouldn't blow a potential sale.

I opened the door and introduced myself. I didn't introduce Merlin—how exactly would I introduce him anyway? Ignoring my pleas, he piped up anyway in his inimitable English accent, making some small talk. The visitors didn't seem to notice anything amiss and Merlin was acting rather casual and relaxed. He wasn't doing any harm, and I figured that perhaps he could charm them or perhaps even encourage the sale of the house. The visitors left without incident and Merlin gave me another knowing wink. Eventually, as fate would have it, these were the people who did buy the house.

The trip to the Yucatan in Mexico was magical. We were not lovers, because of Isaac. But the charge was building and we bonded deeply during this trip. Every minute together was stimulating, adventurous, and exciting.

On our return trip, Joffrey and I jumped onto an earlier flight than the one for which we had originally been scheduled. The flight began smoothly enough but we soon encountered horrendous turbulence. As I was reaching for the vomit bag in the seat pocket in front of me, I heard Merlin's distinctive voice, "Hello, Anamika, do you feel sick?"

I looked over at Joffrey, and sure enough, there was Merlin in his body. He snatched the bag from me and stuffed it back in the seat pocket. "You won't be needing that. You were booked on the later flight to avoid this turbulence, but now that you are here..."

Merlin spread out his arms like airplane wings, took a deep breath, and closed his eyes to increase his focus and concentration. Within seconds the plane began to stabilize. My stomach relaxed.

"That was a great trick, Merlin. I appreciate the help, believe me. I'll have to try it myself sometime," I said. On the next leg of the flight we hit more turbulence and I tried the trick. Sure enough, Merlin's magic worked.

Once back home, I began to let go of my career, my life in Massachusetts, and the security of my relationship with Isaac. Joffrey joined me periodically in Sakkara, which I was still offering several times a week. Being together in this way was wonderful for both of us.

The energies became so intense between us that it was virtually impossible to stay away from each other. Not only did the tension have to break, but also we needed to express the electricity and passion between us. Simply touching each other took us both directly into the most ecstatic Love and opened our energy systems so wide that there were no words. Energetically and physically entwined for hours we journeyed through doorway after doorway into dimensions previously unknown to us.

While I was soaring in my relationship with Joffrey, I felt wrenching conflict about Isaac and battering guilt about the many inelegant ways I was handling the separation. I was so frightened about my upcoming move that I made a big mistake.

I had wanted to end my relationship with Isaac gracefully and with integrity. Instead I betrayed him by sleeping with Joffrey. Yes, one sweet afternoon, we finally made love. Being with Joffrey in this way was beyond anything either one of us had experienced. One could barely label it a sexual experience because it went so far beyond anything we could put in that category. Joffrey and I were not the only ones present in our experiences with each other. There was so much energy from other realms pouring through both of us, and so many beings participating that it was like making love with him and all of existence at once.

However, I had never betrayed anyone before and was mortified by my behavior. In fact, I was so plagued with guilt and shame that I couldn't forgive myself. Although I had wanted to be with Joffrey more than anything in the world, I wished I had ended things cleanly with Isaac first. Looking for relief and a more clear perspective than only guilt, I broached this sore subject with Merlin.

Merlin had generously stayed in Joffrey's body after a Sakkara expressly so that I could speak with him. He turned to me and whispered that I should stay seated with him until everyone had left because he wanted to have a few words with me. He knew I was plagued with guilt. I was relieved to speak with him, but terrified he would blame me as I was blaming myself for jumping in too soon with Joffrey.

Even though I hadn't wanted to hurt Isaac in this way, being with Joffrey was too compelling. Ascended Masters were always jumping in and out of his body day and night, waking me up to give guidance or coming through Joffrey for intense lovemaking. There was no way to resist this astounding magic and beauty.

"Oh, Merlin, I feel like I'm doing a very poor job during this transition time. I'm falling into the fear of letting go and therefore not completing with Isaac as quickly and easily as I think I should. I'm terrified because I'm leaving Isaac and mortified that I've betrayed him—even though we are shifting our relationship. I'm making a huge mess! When I'm this fearful I loose sight of the big picture that everything is all right. Then I really feel unsafe.

Even though I've put the intimate part of my relationship with Joffrey on hold until I move, I haven't forgiven myself. I keep blaming myself with thoughts like, 'If only I could do it better I would have figured out how to have a true partner by now.' Or, 'I should be perfect enough to never make mistakes or hurt anyone. I'm so stupid and weak and it's all my fault.'"

Merlin assured me that I was cleaning up and completing with my past. He also assured me that even though this was a steep path, I was strong enough to meet the challenge and I would be greatly benefitted by having made it through.

I persisted, "I can't understand what happened, I just felt compelled and even pushed to be with Joffrey. What was pushing me? Was it all my fear? I felt no control over my actions. I am terrified because I have betrayed Isaac even after promising that I would always be honest with him."

What Merlin disclosed was shocking to me. He said that the incident had been instigated partly by my fear, but just as much by him. He had pushed Joffrey and I to get involved because the energy between us was so intense that he knew it would break apart some ancient blocks in all three of us. It was his attempt to have us all face some old issues we were all avoiding.

Joffrey and I were very sensitive and impressionable, and I felt angry, betrayed and confused that he had pushed us like that. While it was beyond wonderful being with Joffrey, I wished I had ended things cleanly with Isaac first. It was only later that I both remembered that I had given spirit carte blanche to help move my life forward in whatever ways they saw fit. Later, I also came to see the wisdom of their action. Eventually, I was grateful because we all grew immensely, and in the end, I was able to part gracefully with Isaac.

I was dreading uprooting my whole life in the impending move. On the outside I acted as if I were fine, but on the inside I felt totally irrational as old emotional patterns surfaced. The terror that had come up when I lost my appointment book paled in comparison to this. Now I had to let go of my entire life as I had known it. Talk about overwhelming! I knew I wanted to do it, yet was humiliated to see my fears create such a mess. I had always prided myself on self-control and integrity. Here I was sloshing in the sewer.

To make matters worse, I knew Joffrey and I would not be in a romantic relationship for long. Our personalities were too divergent, so that even though on a spiritual level we were totally one, we could never make it together long term. It was just too stressful on a personal level. We didn't really have the ability to talk things through sufficiently. I couldn't accept where he was coming from and he couldn't accept my point of view. We were like proverbial oil and water or chalk and cheese; we just didn't mix.

During our brief chat, Merlin commented that most awakened beings are in relationships with people who are their complete opposite. During this whole conversation, he befriended me in a way that was so personal, by sharing his own past relational difficulties, that I felt deeply comforted. Apparently, when he was forty, he fell in love with a thirteen year old and ended up murdering her boyfriend in a jealous rage. I was relieved I hadn't resorted to that and was deeply moved that I had made a new close friend.

By framing the situation as part of my soul's lessons, Merlin helped me feel more at peace about the triangle with Joffrey and Isaac, and about my impending move. When I realized how much I was growing through each of these lessons, no matter how messy and imperfect, I could see the potential of relaxing the gut-wrenching knot in my stomach that had persisted for months. The growth was a blessing for which I would be forever grateful. Yet I needed to find some serious self-forgiveness.

In even considering the possibility of forgiveness, some momentary peace descended. If I could only hold that peace until the day I was scheduled to drive away from my old life in two weeks and into my new one. Isaac would be accompanying me to Florida by car, then flying back home. That would be the official ending of our relationship and that day was coming all too soon.

CHAPTER 15

finding forgiveness

Once I had committed to the move, many synchronous events occurred. Since I had first seen the vision of the white crystalline sands in Sarasota, I knew that was where I would be going. My parents had just moved to Sarasota and my mother gave me the name of her realtor. One morning I felt something pressing me to call the realtor now, NOW! I picked up the phone immediately and called.

I described my vision of the white beach cottage and said that it had to be a place that would take a dog. She replied, "I'm sorry, I have nothing like that. That's going to be really difficult to find because most places don't take dogs."

At that exact moment, a woman walked into the real estate office and announced that her beach cottage had just become available and that pets were okay. The realtor described the property to me. It matched my vision perfectly. "That's it!" I said, "I'll take it."

I had already sold my house and furniture. What I hadn't sold I now gave away. The only things I kept for Shamuki were his bowls, leash, and flea comb. I kept my computer, clothing, and car. I let everything else go.

It all happened so quickly. No sooner had I decided that I would follow my vision than the world I had constructed began to unravel. It was as if everything was arranged to move me forward.

Before I knew it, the day of the move arrived. The sky was overcast and a light drizzle was falling. The grayness reflected my inner mood exactly. I had chosen this path even though I had no idea what this move would bring. Leaving everything behind was not as easy as I naively thought it would be. It hurt.

I had packed the car and my house was empty. I took one last walk around the yard, remembering how this home had sheltered us for seven years. Now I was letting it go so that it could hold someone else while I went to a place I had only seen in a vision.

Isaac was waiting by the car to drive to Florida with me. I felt a deep pain that I would soon be letting go of him permanently, as well as my friends, my community, my work, and the town I had cherished for twenty-two years. Overwhelmed with sadness, I wanted to collapse on the damp ground and cry forever. Shamuki nudged my hand, urging me to leave. There would be time to cry in the car.

The drive with Isaac was enough peaceful between us, but emotionally wrenching for me. We had already thoroughly discussed what had happened with Joffrey and were more focused on getting to Florida and on our impending separation than on rehashing the breach. He had found enough forgiveness to be able to accompany me on this trip. I was truly grateful for his caring presence.

After three days on the road, we arrived at the beach cottage. It was as beautiful as the vision. Newly renovated with white stucco, it was situated on a magnificent two million-dollar estate. Its vaulted ceilings framed colorful stained glass windows. A plush green lawn rolled down to a

private, white crystal sand beach fronting a sparkling aqua ocean.

The trees were laden with figs, oranges, grape-
fruits, limes, lemons, and bananas. There was every kind of tropical flower you could imagine and
then some. A wooden footbridge spanned a pond
filled with plump, well-fed coy fish. Completing
this tropical paradise was an artistically sculpted
asymmetrical swimming pool.

The cottage provided a cozy nest. It was quite
small but pristine and lovely. As it was already
furnished with floral prints and rattan, there was
nothing more needed. I set up my computer, positioned Shamuki's bowls, hung up his leash and
my clothes, and that was that. I was ready to go.
But where?

Isaac stayed for several days, providing a welcome
delay to letting go of our relationship. Even though
we had discussed what had occurred with Joffrey
many times while we were still in Boston, we spent
more time reviewing the situation. Again, as I had
done in Boston, I apologized to him profusely. He
listened, but had hardened his heart, probably

more in preparation for the impending separation than only about Joffrey.

I totally understood, but it hurt. Despite that, putting him on the plane back to Boston was one of the most difficult things I ever had to do. It was final; our relationship was over. The separation was something I had chosen, yet had been so afraid to face.

As soon as he was out of sight I felt utterly and inconsolably alone. I walked out of the airport in a haze of grief to find my parked car. Fumbling for my keys, I managed to climb into the car before the floodgates sprang open and I fell into a dark abyss. It was all I could do to take the next breath. I was wailing, "Please help me make it through this transition!" I understood the feeling of not being able to make it through.

Isaac had been a warm, comforting presence and emotional support for three years. I had grown attached to him. Even though I realized that some of the pain was from breaking co-dependent attachments to him it still hurt, and I had to grieve.

I spent eight to ten hours for the first few days sobbing, like in facing a death. I was begging for help just to take the next step. The grief and the terror that arose were about more than just Isaac. I was grieving letting go of my whole life in Boston and the person I had been. I could see why people reached for alcohol or drugs to numb the pain. But I had come too far to go that route. I would have to rely on Shamuki and my own inner resources, and I needed both of them in large doses.

Day after day, I sat on the cool, tiled floor of my cottage with a box of tissues. Shamuki would come over and minister to me. He would lick me, put his paw on my heart, nuzzle in, put his front legs around my shoulders and hug me tenderly.

Sometimes he would just sit across the room and look at me. Often he would sigh, put his head down on his paws and look up periodically letting me know that he was there for me. He patiently waited for me to move through the pain. He never let me out of his sight, attending to me constantly whether he was sleeping or awake. Sometimes he'd say, "Okay, let's go outside, that's enough for now." He'd drag me out with him to walk on the beach.

He made me move, even when I didn't want to and I did feel better after walking a bit.

Several weeks passed in this way. I gave myself permission to face all the feelings that arose, no matter how painful. Shamuki and I covered every inch of the sparkling beach backwards and forwards many times. Playful dolphins came into the cove to befriend us. The pelicans and egrets watched from a nearby wooden pier until he lunged into the surf and scared them away. Despite the beauty of nature and of these gentle beings, I felt desolate, alone and inconsolable.

Joffrey was the one person I wanted to reach for, but he was purposely keeping away after one conversation about our differences. Despite these differences he wanted to be together. But I wasn't able to be in a relationship in which we couldn't talk things through—and he didn't want to do that. So now, he was pushing away while I was in the deepest agony of separation and reaching out to be closer. We had seen each other only once briefly during the past few months. Our lovemaking was once again exquisite, but other than that he was emotionally and physically far away.

Finally, on my birthday, he called me. I heard Miriam's voice speaking through him.

"I feel a lot of pain right now," I cried into the phone.

She reminded me that I was looking to fill an old hole with something else and was trying to become perfect enough to do so. She suggested that I forgive myself deeply for that and continue the process of surrendering into my connection with God.

Miriam was right. Even though I knew better intellectually, I still had the feeling that I needed to be perfect to be loved. I drove myself incessantly to perform everything correctly, instantly, and perfectly.

"Do we just constantly learn lessons? Are you learning lessons too?"

When she assured me that everyone is always learning, I began to understand more about perfectionism. I saw how it demands that we arrive at a place that is perfect, or finished. But we are always learning and growing, and so is all of existence, including God/Goddess/All-That-Is.

"Then why do I have this notion that I have to achieve a state of perfection?"

She explained how perfection was born of our survival instincts and how competition rather than cooperation was hardwired into humanity at this time. It is a rigid closed system, not a fluid open one, she explained. It's one which is imbedded in the current world paradigm. Our current belief system is terribly outdated, she went on, confusing perfectionism with spirituality.

How right she was. And if I couldn't allow myself to make mistakes and find forgiveness, how could I ever truly feel loved since I would never be perfect? I needed to be loved with all of my imperfections and flaws. I began to understand the importance of forgiveness and began to focus more on that than on trying to be perfect.

The less I strove for perfection, and the more forgiveness and acceptance I brought forth for myself, the less defensive I became. I had been rigidly defending myself against admitting my imperfections to others and incessantly reviewed them internally. This left me defensive and inflexible. I began to soften the hardness of the protective layers and found myself feeling more safe and able to gently and safely interact with people.

I could see more clearly how I was projecting my image of perfection onto a man. From that perspective, no man was ever good enough and neither was I. As Miriam had said, this perspective was definitely hardwired in me and was the nature of the world paradigm, as well.

I had arrived at another important doorway of not only forgiving myself for my imperfections, but more importantly forgiving myself for having created those impossible standards, then beating myself up when I inevitably fell short of them. Then I beat myself up for believing that I had to be perfect in the first place! What a cycle!

My idea of forgiveness at this point was that I had indeed done something wrong, but blessedly I could be forgiven and then all would be well. I later understood it to mean that I could see the beliefs that were causing my suffering, and I cared enough about myself to open beyond those limiting beliefs. Each time I would engage my heart in caring about myself or someone else, I found sensations and emotions that were soft and warm. As I felt this softness, I opened. The harshness of my self-judgment was beginning to lift. I reminded myself daily to feel the tender openness of my own heart.

undoing

I was living in a tropical paradise by the sea and yet I was depressed. I had left my career, Isaac, my house, most of my belongings, and my community. I had thought that letting go of so much would make my life better. I had released so many burdens—as well as nurturing connections—and had nothing to bind me or hold me. I had taken this big step based on what "felt right." The vision of the new space was so sparkly and fully of Light that I assumed I would feel that way right away. I didn't realize it was what I would grow into. "I should be happy," I admonished myself. Yet I was suffering from loneliness and despair.

I decided to inquire into this, because the same old feeling was always present and never changing. I went deeper into the perception of separation, the place in which I felt utterly alone, empty and bereft. Each day I thought I should have gotten through the worst of these feelings and that it should be getting better now. Yet, the next day I felt even more lost, alone, desperate, terrified and confused.

I had never before had the courage to fully face the bottomless pit within me and acknowledge its depths. I had never faced how utterly terrified I was simply to be alive when I felt disconnected. I had been covering up this isolated place inside with overwork and distractions. Now I had no distractions, no lover, no friends, no community, and even Joffrey had pulled away from me again since my birthday several months ago.

Thank goodness for Shamuki. He would slow down to walk at my pace if I were particularly vulnerable that day. Sometimes he'd try to get my attention by pointing to things in nature or trying to engage me in swimming or playing. When I went through crying jags he would press up against me providing comfort in his endlessly patient way.

No matter what the situation, Shamuki tried to give me perspective, healing, and companionship. His compassion was beyond comprehension. He lived in the place in which I yearned to be, and he kept gently encouraging me to come and meet him there. He was deeply at peace with life and

himself, a living example of unlimited and unconditional love, serenity and grace.

When Shamuki met people on our walks, he would
light up and open up to communicate with them.
Astounded, I would watch him. I'd feel myself
contracting at the presence of another human,
while Shamuki expanded. The contrast was stark.
I got to see how rejecting I was of just existing, of
being human. On the surface, anyone meeting me
would say I was an outgoing, open, and communi-
cative person. While that was true, what I shielded
from them was an icy, frozen core.

I think that it was really a fear of judgment and
imperfection, and therefore a fear of being deeply
known. Simultaneously, I felt the constant yearning to be vulnerable enough to be fully seen and
loved. I told myself the story that if I opened to be
loved that deeply, I'd either lose myself, be judged,
or be trapped.

Thus, I felt the need to gird myself and hold tightly to my known sense of individuality. However, in
so doing I closed off to emotional intimacy. I repeatedly seesawed back and forth in relationships

between openly connecting and constricted self-protection, keeping people at arm's length.

I later realized that even though I projected this duality of loss of self or of being trapped on human relationships, the source was much deeper than that. I had built up a sense of individuated identity over what seemed like eons, and I was zealously guarding and possessing it as my source of safety. I was treating this part of me as "The One" and only one, and couldn't yet see it as a valuable and integral part of a greater whole.

I began to see how this part of me that was fiercely independent was the one with the distinct point of view on both sides of the same coin. Either, it will be engulfed and consumed by the larger me and therefore lose itself, or it will be trapped and suppressed by a power bigger than it is.

While these fears were valid from the smaller one's point of view, I found that the more I expanded into the larger one which was filled with compassion, the more the smaller part felt angry and threatened that I was leaving it behind because I was beginning to not identify with it so thoroughly.

I was searching for the balance where I could both know myself as me and as one with All—even and especially when in a romantic relationship. I both yearned for and was afraid of love that was so intimate that I would be cherished and adored in every fiber of my being. The lack of what I longed for most was also the source of my agony. Ultimately, I couldn't accept that this dichotomy was the human dilemma.

I suppose I had hoped that Joffrey would fill the void, or that I would be somehow rewarded for my risky move to Florida. Neither was the case. What I did get to experience was more of me, and certainly not my favorite parts.

Since I could no longer find an identity through anything external—from Joffrey to my work—I had the chance to surrender more and more deeply into my inner Source. This was the only lasting source of safety and love. I was seeking that inner peace and security in which I could feel light and free.

To find it required that my old beliefs be undone. "There's more to be undone? Oh no!" Like a flip chart, my mind rapidly reviewed all that I had let go of already. "What more is there yet to undo?" I asked inwardly with horror.

Yet, I knew I was challenging myself to let go into absolute trust. It was a mighty path, but I had come this far and there was nowhere else to go. I surrendered again and again into my internal connection simply through the awareness that it felt better to be open and free.

Gradually, over several months, I began to notice that in fact I was changing. I didn't "do" very much in terms of worldly activities, but instead followed the flow of my own rhythms. I walked on the beach and spent a lot of time in contemplation by the ocean's edge, bathing my senses in its tropical beauty. There was no shortage of entertainment watching dolphins at play, iridescent fish, and Shamuki's antics when chasing egrets. It was a self-prescribed extended vacation in which I was learning to come from a different ground state of being.

Some days were filled with peace and gentle breezes while others were still rugged, rigorous, and painful. On the whole, I could tell that the deep fear that I had been facing was actually being released.

As I began to stop blaming myself for feeling afraid, the independent part began to feel cherished and included, even with its fears. This kind of compassionate understanding helped those fears dissolve.

The pockets of gentle peace I would encounter were soothing. It was the kind of sweet, joyous peace I had longed for and dreamt about. I would have moments, and even hours of feeling in harmony with life, with the world, and with All.

In this state was appreciation for life without gripping, gut wrenching terror. I could breathe deeply without yearning to be somewhere else. I could actually be present with no agenda. There was no desperate need to be touched, met, or filled by something outside myself. Life was full in the moment. I was at peace for no reason, just because I was me and alive, just because I exist.

These tranquil moments would pass and I'd circle through another crying jag. Then I'd go for a walk and a bird would fly overhead. I'd feel its beauty and then instantly I'd be at peace once again. The next moment a wave would lap over my feet and I'd dissolve in tears not only of loss but of joy and gratitude for the magnificence of life.

The waves of life were moving me, washing over and through me. I was so open that I felt every little nuance of life. I had lost my imagined ability to be in control. All I could do was show up for the next moment and keep breathing. I had no ability to make choices, decisions or to think about what I would like to do. There was nothing left other than feeling whatever I was feeling in the moment. I could do nothing but yield to whatever showed up within or around me.

Since I had left behind the external reflections that had given me a sense of identity, I was experiencing life as a free flow of emotions and sensations. This way of living was radically different than the tightly controlled existence I had lived before.

I was in a daily state of undoing, putting one foot in front of the other on faith. Sometimes faith felt to me like gambling everything on nothing. However, in my heart of hearts I knew that faith was really gambling everything on the invisible, larger part of me, which only appeared to be nothing. I increased my trust in the immense paradigm shift I was undergoing.

There is no way I could have prepared myself for the magnitude of the change I was experiencing. There weren't others close by who were undergoing this same sort of undoing. What I was facing was different than what the very few people with whom I was still close were going through. Gabriella was traveling for months at a time, so we were not speaking as often either.

Every time my friends in spirit reassured me that I was in fact progressing, I was uplifted and renewed because from my own point of view, the progress seemed slow. I trusted them more than anyone else. Miraculously, even though Joffrey and I were not seeing each other personally, he was still able to allow spirit to speak to me.

One major source of comfort and support had always been my mother. I was grateful she lived in Sarasota too. However, I no longer felt that she could understand. Increasingly, I was living in some other paradigm of reality. The more I progressed, the more difficulty I was having conversing her.

Rather than being able to connect with what was coming alive in me, she began reflecting the negative judgments I had about myself. She expected me to get over it already. "What's the problem? You're the one who let go of Isaac. Why are you so miserable? He wanted to marry you and you could have done that. Then you'd be living with him and not going through all of these feelings. Why are you not getting over this and getting on with your life?"

I understood that she was concerned for my well-being and wanted me to be happy. But, I knew that what I was going through in terms of a paradigm shift of a whole way of being was much larger than just letting go of Isaac. All that I was feeling was symptomatic of this enormous change.

Being around her would stimulate my own self-judgment and I'd feel desperate to pull myself together and get moving. I'd fall back into thinking that the solution to this situation was an exercise of will and control that ignored the profound feelings that were part of my transformation. I couldn't exercise my will, and she didn't understand that I was opening through veils into other dimensions of reality.

In this new paradigm, it was as if the ease and openness of my very breath were different. It seemed that the quality of the air and the gentleness of my heartbeat had changed. The light filtering through the clouds took on an iridescent hue and sounds contained harmonics. It was like perceiving through different lenses and also sensing life as a flow of energy in and around me, rather than as matter.

Actually experiencing the movement of every moment was completely different than just living. In these states of peace and freedom, old stories and concerns lost their meaning. In fact, there was no superimposed interpretation or striving—only deep joy in experiencing each moment as it was. It was as if all of my senses were open and I was in an exchange with so many dimensions of reality at the same time from the inside out and the outside in.

Although I tried on many occasions to share my experiences with my mother, it quickly became obvious that I couldn't describe my journey in a way she would understand because everything about my new existence was different. What I was experiencing was outside of the world's consensual context so how could she understand something she hadn't experienced?

The longer I dwelled in the new place, the less I could reach back across the dimensions to communicate in a way that anyone, not just my mother, could understand. There was no one around me having the same experiences of dissolution and change.

Joffrey and I couldn't communicate interpersonally because he didn't want to open any more, and I was all about opening ever more fully. He felt threatened by what I was undergoing and wanted to stay "safe." I was looking for authentic lasting inner safety while he was looking for the safety bred of familiarity.

He had had enough growth to suit him and instead just wanted us to be together as we were. When I declined to go that route, he became enraged and shut me out. Even though I knew he was hurt, his stonewalling felt hurtful. He had constructed a huge wall that he refused to deconstruct. Instead, he took refuge behind it and instantly got involved with another woman.

Gabriella told me that every time she mentioned my name he'd begin stuttering or gagging. He so wanted to connect, but just felt too threatened to go where I was going. I understood, because I knew what it took to face the kind of undoing I was going through, but it still hurt that he was no longer in my life on a personal level. Periodically, I still had access to my unseen friends through him.

Other than Shamuki, Joffrey had been the closest person to me. But worse than losing him personally was the thought of losing access to the incredible energies I felt when we were together. That had been my lifeline and I felt like I was hanging on by a thread.

I didn't think I could find those magnificent states of being that we accessed together without him. So that belief had to be undone, too. I grew to learn that the beautiful energies I felt when we connected were not only inside of me, but the very essence of who I am.

CHAPTER 17

the kiss

I dreamed that I was in a place I didn't recognize, filled with people I didn't know. I walked among them, reaching out to connect with someone, but no one seemed to notice me. Then I saw Isaac at the edge of the crowd and ran to him. I touched his arm, "Oh, Isaac, thank goodness it's you! I was feeling so alone, I'm so glad you're here!"

Isaac turned and looked at me with no recognition in his eyes. He shrugged his arm out of my grasp and walked away. Terrified, I ran, pushing through the crowd until I came to a large mirror. I stopped and looked at the person in the mirror with horror. I didn't know this person. Thinking that perhaps this was a trick, I raised my arm and watched the mirror image as I moved. I spoke and watched the lips in the mirror form words. I screamed, shattering the mirror and falling to the ground in a heap, sobbing.

My cries woke me up. I lay still, looking around at the white walls of the beach cottage dappled in sunlight. I recognized the bedspread so I knew I must have put my things here. Where was I? Who was I? My name... what was my name? As hard as I tried, I could not remember my name.

In desperation for some semblance of normalcy, I reached for the phone and pushed the buttons, knowing that it would connect me with someone I knew. The phone was answered by a deep male voice I recognized as Isaac.

"Isaac... Do you know who this is?" I asked timidly.

"Is this a trick?" he asked skeptically.

"No, please," I begged. "I can't remember who I am. What is my name?"

He heard the desperation in my voice and gently replied, "Anamika. Your name is Anamika."

The sound of my name shot through me with a jolt and I remembered my identity. The dream had shown me that I was being made anew and was afraid I would be unrecognizable by losing my identity entirely.

Contrary to this fear, the changes were bringing me into a more peaceful state in which I was continually becoming more of myself, not less. With this reassuring understanding, I felt less vulnerable and I began to venture farther from my cottage. Sarasota had a budding spiritual clientele who frequented health food restaurants, gem shops, and art stores. It was the 1990's and people there were searching for something new. The town had a gentle island feeling. Shamuki and I would go for long walks into town stopping for a break at the bookstore or the juice bar.

During the course of these excursions I began to meet a few people who seemed interested in my work, so I decided to offer Sakkara. One Sakkara turned into another, and soon I was offering several a week. The size of the group constantly grew and my parents attended every one. This was their first experience of the work I did, and while they didn't understand the spiritual aspects, they were fascinated the human psychological parts. They saw people change dramatically, so they couldn't dismiss it even though they didn't fully understand. But who ever does?

I was fine being around people when I was in the group, letting my energy flow. But, I was unable to connect on a personal level with anyone. One day I got a phone call from Christopher, a man who regularly attended Sakkara. "Anamika, it's time for you to be with people again," he said. "How impudent!" I thought. This man has no idea what I'm going through. However, a voice inside told me that he did know. I sensed the wisdom in Christopher's words and I knew he was right. Still, I felt raw, messy and incapable of even having a coherent personal conversation.

A few days later, Christopher called again. "Let me accompany you for a walk on the beach." I consented. Christopher was content to do exactly what he had offered to do, accompany me for a walk on the beach. He was a very easy person to be around. He didn't expect me to talk or tell him anything about my life. He simply walked with me, and of course with Shamuki. It felt good to have another human being with us. After he left, I felt better. I had found a potential friend and some hope that I would eventually be able to enjoy the world again.

Joffrey came to Sarasota to join me in Sakkara. Our relationship had become strained and difficult, yet I still looked forward to working with him again. The work we did together took us to a place so complete, so inspiring and so full. Truly ours was a unique connection. Yet, on a personal level, it just couldn't work. Joffrey didn't stay long; he came to do the work and then immediately bolted. Still, being with him gave me a boost as always.

Sometime after Joffrey's visit I was relieved and thankful to notice that I had begun to feel more at peace. Love was breaking through with a gentle, compelling force. My whole being felt ignited, as if I were connected to the very heartbeat of creation. This love filled me with a golden light that became white, then colorless as its presence radiated out forever.

These experiences were happening more and more often and I was able to sustain them for longer periods of time. I wondered how to hold onto this feeling. I had worked so hard to find it and couldn't bear the thought of losing it over and over again. I just needed to keep focusing on the connection again—something far greater than this old belief in loss.

As I did this more and more, I began to feel I was dissolving again. My old identity was continuing to fall away. I had no thoughts, no desire to do anything, and no place I wished to go. For days on end, my full attention was absorbed by this unusual dissolution.

The sun came up, burned hot with tropical intensity, and went down. The full moon seemed to pulse with echoes of the haunting ancient tribal rhythms I was feeling in my body. I lay in the sun, my skin breathing with its caress, my body undulating with luscious waves of energy as I lay nude in the warm, damp sand of our beach.

Throughout this period I could hardly stand upright because the energy coursing through my body was so potent. However, I could dance. There, alone in my cottage, I danced and danced. The movement of the dance started primal and wild, then evolved into more refined vibrations. Time had no meaning. Everything was now. I kept letting go, letting go, letting go; there was nothing

I wanted to hold onto. I was a vast ocean, a sea of life with passion bursting from my chest.

"God, I love you, I love you. There's nothing but you!" I exulted as wave after wave of exquisite Love poured forth from my heart. I was gently drawn into the arms of God. Tenderly caressing hands pierced through the ethers and came toward me. They stroked my face then ran down the length of my body. I heard God speaking to me softly: "You are my lover, my beloved."

God inhaled and I felt myself physically pulled forward into God's breath. Then God exhaled, breathing energy and life into me through my mouth. The breath of God filled my whole being, recreating me anew. Then God kissed me on the lips saying, "I want all of you with me. Will you be wholly mine forever?"

"Yes, I am yours." I melted further and further.

My breath became the fire of life. Each breath became a spark that ignited into a burning white-hot flame that danced throughout my body until I was ablaze.

"Help me to love you more and more. There is nothing real but this Love."

The identity of who I was had been systematically dissolving. But I could now feel what I was. "I am radiant brilliant Light. No matter what my personal issues are, they are so incidental compared to the brilliant radiant Light that I am!"

For several weeks I floated in this new knowledge of what and who I am. Then I began turning back toward the dark side of the moon. Ascension Day was approaching and the darkness inside of me was intensifying. There was to be a full eclipse of the sun that would perfectly match my feelings. I felt like a puppet. One minute I would be radiantly happy and ecstatic and then, for no apparent reason, I would shift into a mood of dark, bleak despair.

As the time of the eclipse approached, I could feel enormous pressure building inside me. I realized how powerfully I was influenced by not just the moon, but by the movements of all of the planetary and galactic energies. When there was an event like an eclipse, it would sweep over me like a tidal wave and I would have to yield; it was stronger than I was.

I was wedged between the pain brought up by the eclipse and the promise held by Ascension Day. The eclipse tore my heart apart and brought more unresolved wounds to the surface. For twenty-four hours I was in another layer of separation. I felt no hope of ever feeling Love again. The darkness closed in and I wanted to die. Where there had been Love there was now only sadness. Where was the woman who had danced in ecstatic frenzy? That memory seemed like from another era.

I turned inside for answers. "Help me find the Light again," I prayed. I heard the voice of God. "Keep giving your heart despite the pain. Let it tear and break to open new space. It will mend more whole."

"I have nothing left to give you. I am broken down, lost in the ruins of my shattered heart. Help me let go and remember your embrace. Help me know that you dwell in me even here, in this darkest recess."

When the evening came and people gathered for Sakkara, I still felt lost, hopeless and alone. Strangely, as if forecasting something personally intense, I was relieved that my parents were out of town and did not attend this particular event. As we each spoke our desire for awakening that night, I heard my uninspired voice say, "I wish to enter the colorless ray once again and to stay there this time." I had no real hope of this happening, but asked anyway.

The drums began. Soon, the geometric forms of Sakkara and the Ascended Masters in Spirit entered the room. I was so numb and dull that I did not feel connected to Sakkara's energies at all. My only recourse was to let go into my breath and physical movement.

I breathed deeply and stood up. As the drumbeat intensified and my movement increased, the numbness began to melt. Rage arose within me, a wild, primal animal rage. Quickly this rage became so intense that my body could barely contain the energy coursing through it. I found myself in a primitive, tribal frenzy, as if in a trance, possessed by Spirit.

My arms waved about wildly, my muscles pumped with raw animal power. My long, dark curls flew with total abandon and the power flung me onto the floor in a writhing inarticulate heap. All I could hear were silent screams about all of my pain and for all of the world's pain. Rage poured out of each cell and filled my breath.

I defiantly scrambled back onto my feet shouting, "I hate you, I hate you, I hate you!"

It occurred to me for a brief moment that the participants might think I was crazy, but this thought was quickly overwhelmed by the all-consuming feelings. This dance of rage sustained at a wild pitch for over an hour. I had no idea that my body could endure such prolonged frenzied movement.

One by one others joined me until everyone was thrashing about as wildly as I was. As we continued, our passion became more and more inflamed. Each moment seemed to be the height of a fevered pitch. We couldn't imagine a more intense degree of consuming heat. However, just as any given moment's intensity surpassed the last, it too gave way to the next moment's greater inferno.

Then the energies grew even stronger, as if someone had turned up the volume of an amplifier. The room became electrified and charged. My inner voice burst forth in a silent scream that filled my ears and shattered the fabric of our fury. "That's it! I will take no more of this subjugation! I am free to be completely and entirely myself! I am me!"

Millennia of women's oppression and denial of our strength stormed through me. I would not stand for it. I would not stand for reaching for approval outside myself. I would not stand for any renunciation of myself. I claimed that I was beautiful and complete right now. I claimed myself as I had never done before.

As I did, a physical bolt of lightening, which had not come in through any window, flashed and exploded in the center of the room. Bodies scattered right and left, unharmed, just as our frenzy came to a head. The lightening turned from yellow into blue and then white gold, as we fell in exhausted heaps onto the floor. Time stood still as we all slipped into a great void.

I lifted my eyes to see the spot where the lightening had struck. Through the thinning mist I saw an

etheric rectangular frame hovering in the air. Inside its perimeter was another veil. It was as if the
veil that had obscured my connection to myself
had become visible.

I knew that I had a clear choice. I could choose to
enter into Love or remain in perpetual inconsequentiality. Without missing a beat, I accepted this
geometric invitation to step through the window.
I jumped up, flew across the room and stepped
through the frame.

On the other side of the veil there was only white
light. This Light had beckoned and invited me to
merge with it so that we would become one. The
sensation was that of all consuming Love. The
colorless presence of exquisite, unnamable Love
poured through my being and I was home again.

I could see the veil and the window dissolving behind me. Gently, I was ready to bring back into the
room the Love with which I had merged. Everyone
in the room could sense it tangibly. We sat in silent
communion with each other as no one wished to
disturb the sacredness of our experience.

Gradually we broke away, holding our oneness with that Love within ourselves. People slowly left to go home. No one was moving too quickly as we had been powerfully altered by what we had experienced together. When it was time to leave, I wanted to stay close to someone who had experienced this extraordinary evening. So I invited Christopher, who had attended the event, to come back to my cottage with me for a while.

Christopher, Shamuki and I walked on the white sand beach under the new moon, bright stars, reveling in the warm tropical breeze. We wrapped our arms around each other, and offered our feet to the gentle waves. The three of us stood in a silent embrace, surrendered to Source, all three knowing we were of that Source, and each acknowledging it in the others.

We sat on the beach in this magical mood all night. Christopher left early in the morning and I finally lay down to welcome sleep. When I awoke a few hours later, it was a bright, clear morning. I could still feel the divine Love coursing through my body. Clearly something within me had changed. I felt whole and filled with radiant joy.

the gift of compassion

My joy persisted and I was continuously flooded with Love and bliss for weeks on end. In this state, I was drawn more and more to Christopher. We both wanted our relationship to become more intimate. I knew it would not be long-term because there were many levels on which we could not relate to each other, but we had a powerful connection. Christopher understood me spiritually in a way no one else around me did. He could recognize my connection with other realms and could sense and honor my inner work.

My decision to become intimate with Christopher confounded my mother and created a further breach in our relationship. "Have you gone completely crazy? You have a Ph.D. and the man is an idiot! He doesn't earn a speck of money! Why would you want to support a man financially? He dresses like a beach bum and he can't even put a sentence together! What could you possibly see in him?" She wasn't wrong about the fact that on the surface Christopher and I did seem ill suited to each other. But I also knew that there were other reasons that made being together for a time the right decision.

To her consternation, I stood my ground, even though I knew my mother's worldly evaluation was accurate and I valued her opinion. This was a decision I made for myself and it had nothing to do with anyone else. I wanted the healing balm of Christopher's sweetness. While I did explain to her that this was a temporary liaison for my healing, she wouldn't hear of it. She wanted me to have a "real relationship" like I had with Isaac.

Nevertheless, Christopher and I decided to live together as our relationship was soothing to my ravaged nerves and supportive to him. This was truly a happy time in a sweet innocent way. Our days were simple and stress free. I followed my inner impulses in each moment to determine what to do next. Most of my time was unstructured and life seemed to just flow.

We moved into a stucco and glass house on a point of land surrounded by water on three sides. I created a community of friends and family who gathered in our home several days a week for Sakkara. My parents still attended Sakkara and my mother came and cooked lunch for the group. This time was deeply nourishing.

Joffrey and I were still not close and I had to let him go. I was able to give him the space that he needed, realizing that our connection was eternal, even though currently strained. I was still able to speak to spirit through him periodically and I hoped that eventually our personal friendship would return.

To continue the inner work I had been doing, I went to see a healer in Santa Fe. She told me I must give my heart to the world. She said I had been afraid to do this because I had a fear that it would break. "It will," she said, "let it break."

When I returned to Florida, a stabbing pain in my heart had surfaced. Mirroring my inner turmoil, a storm system hung overhead for a week. The whole time it was building in intensity, I was held in suspension waiting for it to break and clear.

Inside of me, mountains of fear and resistance emerged. I was afraid of being on this Earth. I was afraid to allow my heart to truly open with nothing held in reserve and no secret place to retreat for protection. It would take great courage for me to open myself and allow my heart to break even further, but I had no other choice; I had come too far to stop now.

"Okay, I will give my heart completely." Just as I said these words, the thunder began to rumble outside. As the storm's winds raged, the elements helped break my remaining resistance apart. My being tore asunder and split wide open in concert with the clapping thunder and the lightening that streaked to the ground in jagged, tumultuous bursts.

I felt a well-worn cloak of personal history dropping off behind me. Thus unencumbered and cleansed, I was taken into a chamber of pure light used for initiations of the heart. I entered the chamber and opened my heart, "God, I give you everything."

As I said these words a grief welled up in my chest and I wept as I let go of all I had known as myself. The skies burst open with a deluge of rain that flowed in harmony with the torrents of tears that fell upon my chest. I felt laid bare, with nothing left but the knowledge of my essence. From that essence I was Woman, Goddess, Teacher, Lover, Sister, Daughter, and Mother. My heart was the heart of the world.

An almost unbearable compassion flowed through me that made me weep, yet filled me with joy. In this divine feminine energy, I felt strangely yet deliciously unattached to the world while even more present. Paradoxically, in giving forth my heart, I had come to be even more in the world and yet even less of it.

It became clear that compassion was born of sorrow. I had always wished to feel utter compassion for everyone and everything no matter what. "Please help me live from a heart of compassion and give it to the world," I asked beseechingly.

As I uttered this intention, I felt compassion enter my heart with a rush. My heart was full to bursting. This beautiful compassion was my upcoming birthday gift.

As my birthday rolled around, I realized that two years had passed since Joffrey and I had symbolically married God. So much had happened. I did not recognize myself as the same person who had so earnestly made those vows. I had come far and nothing could turn me back now.

Christopher and I were still living in the same house, but we were growing apart. I was changing so quickly, it seemed that I had reached the proverbial point of no return. Nothing was the same. Daily I was opening more into my inner connection and the sole focus of my life had become my journey.

I began to see everything in the context of my journey and symbolic of it, as if the world were a mirror. It reliably showed me a reflection of my expansive changes and constricted places that were calling for attention.

I faced everything just by telling myself the truth about what I was experiencing. And as I did so, I began to sense a momentum and an inner fullness building. My mind jumped to going elsewhere having to do with sharing what I had learned with others. While I did have a true desire to share my gifts, I also had some lingering false notion of having a mission. That was born of a savior pattern in which I took on responsibility for the happiness of others in order to prove my worth.

I couldn't yet imagine living simply for the joy of being me—and how we all naturally impact each other through the luscious pleasure of being ourselves. That kind of freedom came in increments over years.

I was wondering where life would take me next. Joffrey called me once again on my birthday. We sat in silence over the phone not saying much, but reveling in our connection. After our wonderful connection in which I could feel all of our unseen friends, I basked in the glow. Had they hinted that I would be moving soon? I felt so at peace that at the moment the idea of physically moving again did not seem to be a particular challenge. If I were to move, I would.

The doorbell rang, interrupting my musings. To my surprise it was a messenger with a dozen white roses and two birthday cards. I placed the roses in a vase on the table and sat down in front of them to open the cards. One was from Joffrey and the other was from the Chief. Apparently the Chief had jumped into Joffrey's body in the middle of the night, driven Joffrey and his car to a 24-hour store and had selected two cards. The message inside each was very simple, "Anamika, I love you." One was signed Joffrey and the other the Chief.

CHAPTER 19

the double yammy theory

Joffrey came to stay for a week. I was thrilled and hopeful that perhaps we would be closer again. He had softened some of the outer layers of his wall against me but kept the central girding in place. He had come under the pretext of work. However, both of us were feeling a great sense of anticipation, as though a new phase of our lives was about to unfold.

We engaged in the long metaphysical discussions that had become a central feature of our relationship and discovered that both of us had been receiving messages that it was time to move. I told Joffrey that the name Santa Barbara kept popping up. I knew it was in California but I had never been there. I described to him some of the messages I had been receiving.

For instance, one day a drunken, disheveled bum had appeared out of nowhere on the beach in front of my house. He kept beckoning for me to come out and speak with him. He said he had spent the last twenty years traveling up and down the coast of California. I asked him where he thought I should live. "Montecito," he said. "It's a section of Santa Barbara." As I was mulling this over, the man disappeared. One moment he was there, and the next he was gone as mysteriously as he had appeared.

That night I also received a phone call from Gabriella who said she had recently moved to California. She was living in someone's six-million-dollar mansion and insisted that I just had to come and visit. When I asked where in California it was that she lived, she replied, "Montecito, it's a section of Santa Barbara."

The next morning, as I was dressing, a white blouse that I hadn't worn in a long while literally flew off the hanger into my hands. The label, which I had never noticed before, seemed to jump out at me. The name of the clothing company was Santa Barbara.

As Joffrey and I talked, I realized that it seemed like I had been on hold for a year and a half. True, I was doing necessary inner healing work, but I was now ready to begin my life's work again. Inside I was preparing to move on and I could see that the messages to move to Montecito reflected this shift.

With Joffrey there, I got the courage to speak with him about my fears of ending my relationship with Christopher, which I could sense would soon be over. I had been feeling so ambivalent about Christopher. I wanted a different kind of relationship, the kind I had been waiting for my whole life. I knew that Christopher was not this partner. We had given each other a great gift of healing, and now the differences between us that had so extremely exasperated my mother mattered to me, too.

At the same time, I felt incapable of letting him go. As with Isaac, I had become very attached to Christopher—to the point of experiencing fears of loss and jealousy. Even though I was thinking of letting the relationship go, I didn't want to see him with anyone else. This made no sense, except to my jealous and possessive nature.

I was once again giving up a relationship because I had outgrown it. In this way, it was similar to what I had experienced with Isaac. Here were two beautiful men in what were ultimately limited relationships for me. I knew I had to let go.

"What I want, whether it is with Christopher or not, is to experience the depths of that unconditional love within me—and also in relationship," I confided to Joffrey. In saying this I was also interested in seeing whether Joffrey was open to reconnecting in a caring way without having the form be the way he wanted as a marriage.

"I'm so afraid to let go because I don't trust that I'll be brought to something higher. My linear mind knows that every time I have let go—the next relationship, the next house, the next form of my work—always gets better; but I fear that there will not be more, only net loss.

"When the time comes for a change, what if I make the wrong decision? I feel if I make the wrong choice I might never find love and never find God on a deeper level than where I am now, which is fully satisfying only intermittently. Christopher will go off and be with someone else and somehow I will never find the love I want. That's much worse than dying. I'm not afraid of dying, I'm afraid of living without love. Is holding onto this relationship blocking my true soul mate from coming in?"

Joffrey reminded me that I was listening to many old, internal stories about loss of love instead of being present with what I knew to be so. Even knowing that a parting was coming, I decided to settle into the warmth with Christopher that was present now.

About a month later I realized that our lack of harmony had reached the point of no return. It no longer felt right for Christopher and me to have a romantic relationship. However, we still loved each other and wanted to remain close.

We had a veritable conundrum whose resolution would require grace and insight. The fears of making this change seemed overwhelming as I set out to Santa Barbara for my first visit.

Gabriella welcomed me into the fabulous six million-dollar Montecito villa in which she was staying. We continued to be able to read each other with impeccable clarity. She had been with me when I was deciding to part from Isaac and, co-incidentally, she had parted from her partner at the same time. Now, once again, I poured my heart out to her, and she understood it all. I heard in her the clear voice of wisdom speaking to me. Then, much to both of our surprise, our conversation catalyzed in her the awareness that she was actually facing the very same kinds of issues in her relationship that I was in mine.

We spent hours together discussing our respective situations, wondering how we could transmute the pain of impending separation into unconditional love and acceptance. We wanted to be so full within ourselves that we could be 'in love' without attachment to form.

We also wanted to remain close to our partners—even though we no longer wished to be romantically involved with them. Our goal was to get to a place where we could be supportive of these lovely men and both happy for them and at peace within ourselves when they brought in new romantic interests. It was definitely a tall order for my jealous nature—but there was really nowhere else to go.

Gabriella and I cloistered ourselves in the mansion and laughed and cried our way through. Little by little, as each day passed, there were moments of reprieve before the next wave of fear and sadness hit. Revelation after revelation began to replace the pain as we touched our own wholeness within.

I had always believed in unconditional love and had felt many moments of it. However, the fear of loss that permeated my life had prevented me from living that experience consistently. Gradually, as Gabriella and I worked through the maze of our self-limiting beliefs, new experiences of this expansive and unlimited love were starting to occur. I began to feel a greater acceptance of myself—just as I am—and of Christopher, just as he was. It even seemed possible to imagine accepting him in partnership with another woman without needing to shut him out of my life.

Once again, I was going through a death and rebirth into a new being. All I could do was surrender further into the process. As a step along the way, Gabriella suggested that I do a completion ceremony with Christopher in order to state my intentions clearly and to free myself to step through a doorway once again. With all my difficulty around leaving him, this seemed a daunting task but I was determined to find the strength to do it when I returned to Florida.

One thing had become clear to me—the pain I was feeling was actually leading me somewhere. For the past two years during this time of the year approaching Ascension Day I went further into freedom. Clearly, I had not yet been ready to stay in that lightness and inevitably would find myself back in separation after days or weeks. This, the third year approaching this particular day, I intended to stay far longer. I was determined to strengthen my courage and increase my trust.

With my vision now clearly set on moving to Santa Barbara, I found a pool of resentment surfacing. I ranted and raved, "Why do I have to face so much pain? Why can't I have what I want? Why is this so hard?" It was like saying, "Why hast thou forsaken me?"

Then, I turned my anger inward, "How could I be so stupid? How could I allow myself to go through so many years of the same kind of experience over and over and still not 'get it'? Why am I forever subject to the same miserable, limiting emotional responses?" I felt too angry about all of the pain to forgive myself for being where I was. I began beating myself up and heaping on self-blame.

Finally, I asked for help. "Lift this self-hatred and teach me further forgiveness and compassion toward myself. Help me accept my human failings. Help me accept my dark side."

As I asked for this acceptance of my human condition, I could feel the beginnings of a healthy detachment. In this greater freedom, I also began to feel more love toward Christopher. I felt the possibility of truly supporting him on his life path, even thought it would take us apart. What I wanted most was for him to evolve and be happy. That became much more important to me than the form our relationship took.

While I had always believed in this perspective, I began to experience its truth. I saw that the whole play was perfectly orchestrated for this lesson in my growth.

"Please help me resolve my jealous attachments so that I can awaken to unlimited and unconditional love. I recommit myself to this. I will not stop now."

All too soon, after a wonderful week together, it was time for me to go home and face what awaited me. Gabriella and I reluctantly parted at the quaint little Spanish-tiled Santa Barbara airport. We blessed each other on our respective solo flights after having shared so much together. We knew we would be seeing each other soon as it was now clear to me that Montecito would be my next home. While I had trepidation about the upcoming changes and the loneliness I might face, I felt a growing strength and peace within me. Since I had such a deep connection and communication with Gabriella, it was consoling to know I would be spending time with her in Montecito. Knowing she was there was a warm contrast to my wrenching move to Florida.

On the airplane I took a stretch and went into the bathroom. As I turned toward the mirror I saw compassion radiating from my eyes at a level I had never seen in myself before—and it was towards myself. I blinked and opened my eyes to be sure. It was still there. I had changed and grown.

I felt no lack, only inner abundance as I realized that I was not losing anything. I was simply facing the belief in separation that kept me from experiencing the fullness of love. I tentatively allowed myself some morsels of self-appreciation: I had demonstrated tremendous courage and faith, and a deep capacity to experience love.

Somehow I took comfort in these thoughts. It was so fragile, so new to actually feel self-love. Let it unfold gently in its own time, I thought. Simply have gratitude for whatever is now.

A smile crept over my face. I thought, "You know, I could end up wild, crazy in love." Then I realized that the best part is that it would be love for myself—and for no particular reason.

Filled with this warmth, I arrived home. Christopher had moved out while I was away. My first night sleeping alone passed uneventfully. However, the next day old beliefs surfaced about being so completely insignificant and irrelevant that I may as well not exist at all. I wanted to die. As before—I didn't want to kill myself, I just did not want to exist.

This space was black and deep, but within a few short hours, an inner light dawned and I knew I had made it through. I realized that I was not insignificant. I am uniquely me just as everybody else is uniquely themselves. I saw that I had been searching for "the One" to fulfill me outside of myself because I had not realized that even though I was one small part of the Oneness, I was just as valuable and cherished by All as the whole. There was no difference. I saw that there was no one more precious and special than anyone else. There was no hierarchy as we were all important parts of the great Oneness. I simply had not been cherishing myself.

Christopher and I carried out a beautiful completion ceremony in the presence of our caring community. We pledged our eternal love while acknowledging the beauty and importance of the journey we had taken together. In honoring each other, we spoke of our need to go in separate directions, releasing each other in caring. We exchanged strawberry calcite stones to symbolize our bond for stabilizing emotions in the heart. All this was done through many tears and much gratitude.

Fifteen minutes after the ceremony ended I walked upstairs into my bedroom. Christopher was in my bed with one of my students. I immediately kicked them both out of the house. Even though I more than suspected something might happen this way, his actions were my worst nightmare come true. This kind of scenario was the one thing I thought I could not endure; yet I had to face this too. It was both a reflection of my fears and symptomatic of Christopher's emotional immaturity. His actions seemed calculated to hurt me and were contrary to the beauty expressed in the ceremony.

In trying to understand him, I realized that his psyche was too fragile to withstand the separation without holding on to someone else. The alternative to his actions would have been a fracturing in that he didn't yet have the strength to hold his own inner light.

Understanding this helped immensely. Yet the possessive part of me still viewed him as *my* man. I couldn't help but feel that he was being unfaithful to me, even though we had terminated our relationship. The irrational part of me wanted to punish him and to kill her. I asked for help to let go and to experience unconditional love.

In my pain, I never wanted to see Christopher again but my heart would not allow that. I did care about him. I realized that I didn't need to let go of him; I needed to let go of my attachment to him. I was determined to learn unconditional love in the face of my own attachments. I wanted to accept Christopher exactly how he was, not for who I wanted him to be.

This situation was my opportunity to open my heart more. I could feel God's presence intermingled with me so strongly that all I needed to do was focus inwardly. I noticed that as long as I stayed in that Love, all else was handled with ease and the pain was released. If I left that precious connection, then of beliefs of lack, loss, and separation would wrench my guts. The connectedness felt joyous, open, and liberating and I was there, I was home.

I had always wanted to live as an instrument of that Love. As I remembered this desire, it was as if a faucet turned on and I was standing under an open tap. I felt my cells regenerating into new life in the ever-expanding nature of Love.

Later that day in Sakkara, when I looked over at Christopher, tears welled up inside of me because of the loss of him as my lover. The tears were also the grief of having experienced the loss of my own inner connection for millennia. Gently, I leaned into my own heart.

I looked at Christopher again and felt a deep love along with a strange detachment after having been together for a year and a half. I could truly see him for who he was without projecting an image onto him of who I needed him to be. I knew that I would care about this man forever even though we couldn't continue on in the old way. There was peace in letting go. A sweet compassion infused the room and Sakkara ended tenderly.

Several of us stayed afterwards when suddenly something very strange occurred. Mid-sentence, I found myself in a state in which my personality self disappeared. Aside from a fleeting concern that I might have gone crazy, I was not afraid even though my personality self was nowhere in sight. It was as if I was pure consciousness. I had no emotions, no concerns, no thoughts, nothing. I just was. I could vaguely remember having had a personal history, but I had no connection with it and no feelings about it. The story was irrelevant. My identity, Anamika, no longer existed in that moment. I was in the world, but utterly detached from it.

As I was noting all of this, someone looked at me and called my name. I heard myself reply, "That's not my name."

"What is your name, if not Anamika?" she inquired, quite frankly puzzled.

"I don't seem to have one at this moment," I replied. The people who had stayed gradually left after I reassured them I was okay. I lay on my bed in this state all night simply observing what was occurring. Shamuki watched over me. When morning broke I felt my consciousness gently reintegrating with my personality self. Surprisingly, I was relieved to have Anamika back. "I kind of like her," I thought, "despite all of her quirks."

More importantly, I felt gratitude for this human self, which was an expression of part of my larger consciousness. While I felt more appreciation for being human, simultaneously there was a greater detachment from the drama. Gradually, over the next several days as I became more comfortably reintegrated in my human self, new lessons began to appear.

One morning I awoke angry. When I delved into it, I discovered that I had been judging and making myself wrong for my feelings, emotions, and inner processes. "Who says it's better to feel joy than sorrow? Who says it's wrong to feel fear?" I asked myself. For a moment in time I suspended all judgment and then thanked all of my darkness as well as my light. I dared to accept all of me.

The crippling self-rejection and self-judgment were again suspended and suddenly, in their place was an inexpressible joy and freedom. This is it! This is it! In a flash I had understood that I was completely fine the way I was. There was no need to be any other person, or any different than who I was, how I was, or where I was in my process.

I began to repeat, "I am who I am. I am where I am." Soon I was singing a childlike song, "I yam who I yam. I yam where I yam." This little child was singing a truth about life, her Double Yammy Theory, which included both who and where "I yam." I laughed, promising her that I would remember that her Double Yammy Theory was the key to a joyous existence.

extraterrestrial encounters

Day by day I was surrendering more and more into my inner Light as I was finishing up my stay in Florida. In contrast to this Light, from which I derived inspiration and motivation, I could more easily sense where I was continuing to hold on to my personality's desires ambitions. These drives caused me to try to push ahead of where I was. I could identify the frustrated constriction those demands produced. They stood out in stark relief to the lightness, freedom and joy I had been experiencing. I kept reminding myself that growth was a process, not a state of perfection.

As I entered the lightness more deeply I began to have visits from the same ET's who had first come to me several years ago in Boston. Back then, as I was sitting on my living room couch pondering the nature of existence, I was startled by an etheric presence appearing before me. I would have been frightened by this quite human-looking ET, but he was infusing me with such love that I relaxed. Under five feet in stature, with shoulder length dark hair, his face resembled my own to an uncanny degree that was shocking. He spoke telepathically directly into my consciousness as clearly as if he were speaking aloud.

He said his name was Yahweh, and was an Eloha, the singular of the ET group called Elohim. He was one of the physically immortal Elohim. He went on to say that Elohim—meaning "they who came from the stars"—were considered by many other groups to be an extremely intelligent life form.

He said that their technology is approximately 25,000 years ahead of ours and they clone themselves to achieve physical immortality. He spoke for a long time about how the Elohim created Earthlings and formed our planet into a place that would support life. The stories written in the Bible, he went on to say, were about the Elohim and about himself, Yahweh, but they got misinterpreted as mystical rather than practical events. That included mistaking the name Yahweh and Elohim for God. It appeared to the humans of the day that these comparatively advanced beings were

Gods. As he spoke, he filled in so many missing pieces for me about our human history, cosmology in general, and my personal life—including my relationship with him. I felt like I had found my true father at last. One simple example was that what was written in the Bible as the "burning bush" were the lights of his spacecraft landing near that bush. The parting of the Red Sea was done by their wind and laser technology.

As Yahweh took a breath to allow me to integrate what he was saying, I had a flashback about a different group of extraterrestrials I had been in contact with several years before. They were bluish in color and were equipped with a laser technology capable of performing miraculous healing work.

I had first encountered these beings while I was in a contemplative state with my eyes closed. Suddenly a female presence appeared before me. I felt great warmth radiating from her, yet I was frightened by her unfamiliar physical form. She was a shimmering bluish color with large but gentle dark eyes and four insect-like appendages. When she indicated that she would like to work through me, I felt wary. What if I get abducted? What if I let her into my body and can't get her out?

She remained before me, calm and loving, repeating her request. I felt her compassion and caring and was moved to consent. She descended into my body through the top of my head. In the past, whenever other beings such as Ascended Masters came into my body or blended energies with me, the entry was smooth because they were in human form like me.

When these beings in spirit came to me, I didn't leave my body and channel for others like Joffrey did. Instead, I could feel their energy within me and hear their voices speaking within my consciousness. Even though I could access them to a certain degree myself, when they came through Joffrey it was extremely helpful to me, just like talking to a friend who could give a different perspective than I myself had.

When this blue ET came into my body, I was poked and jabbed by her angular limbs and joints. After a lengthy series of maneuvers to adjust the fit, she was comfortably seated in my body.

She began to fill me with a deliciously sweet and fragrant essence. I relaxed. Then she pointed her long, bony fingers through my shorter, fleshier ones, sending laser beams through them. Each finger, she explained telepathically from inside my head, is used for a different frequency and color of beam. The different beams serve different purposes. For example, some are for dissolving blockages, some for healing wounds, some for mending bone, some for bringing peace and some for raising one's overall vibration.

Excited by the possibilities of using this new technology, I played with shooting beams out my thumb and other fingers until I became proficient. When it was time for her to leave, the exit process was as awkward and arduous as the entry. She indicated that if we practiced this many times it would become easier. I was curious to see what the results would be and whether I could continue this on my own after the training.

The next day I enlisted Gabriella as a test case to see what the lasers could do. As I was standing by my healing table, I invited in the extraterrestrials. This time three bluish shimmery beings appeared—one female and two males. One of the males indicated that he would like to help. We went through the several minute awkward entry process after which he performed laser surgery on my friend.

They increased Gabriella's vibration by filling her with energy all over and pointed their lasers into her organs. I had the impression that they were dissolving what looked like dark cysts in various organs. She reported perceiving the male ET's presence and experiencing great warmth from him. Afterwards, she felt much lighter all over and particularly in her organs, even though she wasn't sure exactly what had happened.

My next challenge was presented when I was asked to offer the laser healing of the extraterrestrials for a group of thirty people. Even though I had warned the group that the entry would take a while, I felt embarrassed sitting there in dead silence for five minutes while a blue female ET came into my body. Finally, the fit was complete, and she instructed me to stand up and walk around the room, transmitting her warmth and healing energies through my hands and eyes.

All was going well until I heard a high pitch sound like "weeeeeew" in my head. She indicated that I should let this sound come out of my mouth. Now

I was really embarrassed. Despite this I let go and an ongoing series of high-pitched sounds came out of my mouth and persisted for the duration of the healing.

When the healing portion of the program was complete and the ET had lifted out of my body, I looked around the room with great trepidation, fully expecting to be run out of town. The room was dead silent which only confirmed my negative expectations. I nervously began, "Uh, I, uh, have never done this before, so I, uh, could use some feedback."

One woman immediately raised her hand and promptly burst into tears. She said that she had been in a severe car accident ten years prior in which her pelvis had been shattered and never properly healed. As a result she lived with chronic pain and a severe limp. She said that she had seen a long list of doctors over those ten years and they had finally given up on her saying that there was nothing they could do. She reported that during the healing she felt a ball of warm light enter her pelvis in the exact location of the shattered bones and the pain left instantly. When she stood up and walked to the bathroom, she realized that not only was the pain gone, but there was no more limp!

Several other people that night reported "miracle" healings of cataracts and various ailments. Others reported seeing lights, laser beams, colors, and feeling embraced by great compassion. One well-known clairvoyant in the room described the ET exactly as I had seen her. Her validation was greatly reassuring to the part of me that still thought I had made all of this up.

The voice of Yahweh speaking to me telepathically brought me back from recalling these events of several years prior. Now, here was Yahweh still standing before me. He asked if I'd like to take a trip with him back to our home planet to see our house and my room. I was thrilled, and the next thing I knew I was out of my physical body, traveling in his spacecraft. He wanted to show me how the material and control panel responded to touch and thought.

When we arrived I was shocked! The round beds with furs, the pink squirrels, the cloning labs, and the flowers that produced scented music had appeared in my dreams for years. This first of many subsequent journeys with him was brief, and before I knew it, I was back in my body. Only a few minutes had elapsed.

This encounter was so profound that it began a series of miraculous changes. I had no idea where any of it would lead. So I let go of trying to understand what was occurring because I was experiencing the deepest sense of home I had ever known.

Around this time I also began to experience myself on other planets and as part of different ET groups as well as in many different bodies on Earth. It was all going on simultaneously, and the notion of past and future changed meaning. Since it was all happening now, I could see that Anamika was just one tiny expression of the whole of who I was.

I kept surrendering, putting myself into God's hands over and over again. I could also see that when God came to me through Yahweh it was beautiful and special, yet I also had my own direct connection. While Yahweh was our "creator god" on Earth, he was not God. I cherished Yahweh as a beloved, but I didn't falsely idolize or worship him, or confuse him with the greater whole.

As I surrendered to God directly, revealing my heart, I was lifted into a freedom so light and joyous that I smiled and laughed. As Love poured through me I could sense that all that mattered was to be myself and honestly admit what I was experiencing. As I was present with all of me, I felt the bliss of liberation. Nothing mattered—it was all Love.

CHAPTER 21

my beloved

Just as synchronicities had quickly moved me from Boston to Sarasota nearly two years before, the same magic moved me to California. When I first arrived in Montecito, I was mesmerized by its beauty. My house was a mountain retreat with an expansive view of the ocean. Shamuki and I hiked the steep, windy trails and spent much time outdoors, just breathing in the wonder of it all.

When I had moved to Florida, part of my family lived there and before long I also had friends—Christopher, and a committed group of students. I had quickly built a community and was eventually almost as busy as I had been in Boston. Apparently, at a certain point I thought I had been idle long enough and began to recreate my life.

Here in California I was beginning at square one all over again. I knew no one but Gabriella, who was soon to move on to New Mexico after her brief stay in Montecito. Despite all of the deep inner change, I thought that because I had let go of Christopher and was coming to California clean and clear, my true soul mate would appear.

Soon I began looking for him everywhere. The old familiar terror began rising in me again and I had the grave realization that I was not as clear as I had thought. "Oh no, not again," I moaned as the constant crying began again.

I began to realize that I was facing much more than the loss of Christopher and my Florida community. I was in another step of shifting from one paradigm, one way of being, to another. The change was so intense, it was akin to saying goodbye to life on Earth and moving to another planet, like the ones I had visited with Yahweh and during other journeys in consciousness. When I was in expanded states I would suddenly find myself in different dimensions of reality.

While arguably this change into a lighter, freer way of being is a preferable one, this kind of shift was extraordinarily challenging to undergo. Day by day, I could feel myself being recreated. It was like being released from prison and dying to the self I had been. While I craved this new freedom with my heart and soul, I was also scared as I was being remade anew yet again.

Throughout this process, every day I got to face what needed completing, forgiving and letting go. I was helping others do the same as I began attracting new clients. Sharing the process helped me feel not so crazy and alone.

I began to see that my pain was taking me deeper into Source. Each day I surrendered more and more of who I had thought myself to be. Each day I examined my motives and identified the fear-based ones, asking for help with those, and wishing to be helpful to others. The aloneness gradually gave way to a gentle sweetness, peace, and joy. I was delighted and felt that I had finally arrived at a real beginning.

Confidently, I requested, "Take anything and everything standing in the way of unconditional love." A pain seared through my heart so strongly that I became engulfed with what seemed like the pain of all existence.

There was nothing I could do to lift it. I screamed at God all day and night, "How can you allow this pain? How could you have done this to me if you say you love me? How do you expect us to live in this hellhole called Earth? Don't you care how we feel? I need your caring and compassion now!" I demanded.

Gradually I shifted from being the victim of the pain to the owner of all the pain in the world. "All of this darkness is in me." I finally conceded. "I contain revenge, deceit, dishonesty, depravity, jealousy, betrayal, seduction, thievery, possessiveness, lust, desire, greed, insanity, hatred, manipulation, arrogance, superiority, inferiority, insecurity, demands, control, distrust, pride, guilt, violence, war... I have it all, everything but murder in this life. Oh, what am I saying, I just killed a flea this morning. Yes, murder too. So what if I haven't killed a human in this life, I have vengeful feelings of wanting to kill and I remember killing in other lives. I regularly kill myself with violent, punishing self-hatred, so yes, I have it all! There's no darkness I do not have. I have been denying this all of my life. And if you can love me even now with all of this you are bigger than I am!" I completely disarmed myself by chuckling aloud as this last sentence came out of my mouth.

As I accepted my darkness, I found a freedom in admitting it all. Surprisingly it ceased to feel badly. Yet, it didn't feel good either. I realized that I was suspended in the center between light and dark. In this suspended state, nothing mattered that had driven me up until then—not my lifelong quest for God consciousness, and not even the search for my soul mate, which I had often placed as primary in importance. None of it mattered, not in the slightest. I felt like a clear pane of glass. My needs, desires, attachments, and life as a person were not present as I sat suspended as no thing in nothing.

In this state, I did not think at all of myself. It was my greatest joy to give to others. I could now feel that the more love I gave, the more I had. My self-centered concerns did not exist here.

On an impulse I opened the front door. There was a beautiful large yellow and black butterfly on the straw mat. It seemed to be dying. The butterfly's spirit rose up and was transformed into a large angel who seemed to be a validation that I had indeed gone through a transformation.

As the spirit left the body of the butterfly and it physically died, I picked it up and gently carried it into the house with gratitude. A corner had been turned. While there was more to come, something had irrevocably changed.

For a while, I felt more powerless than I had before. I came to admit that there was truly nothing that I as a person could do separate from my connection with Source. My finite self was too limited to ever attain either happiness or fulfillment all by itself. It was actually a relief to keep admitting my powerlessness and not try to build it back up to have some kind of power over anything. When I admitted the emotion of powerlessness, I would relax into myself deeply from which place I could access my true power, which was a state of being of consciousness. This true power then flowed through my body as energy, awareness, and creativity.

Then I had a conversation with Gabriella in which she said that she sensed that my soul mate was coming and that it would be soon. Given that she tended to be quite "psychic" this sent me reeling. After the initial shock and excitement wore off, I was plagued with doubts. I became deathly afraid that it would never happen. Even if he did arrive he would never want me. I wasn't good enough, smart enough, or attractive enough. Every insecurity about myself surfaced yet again, including long forgotten childhood ones.

I dared to dive below these insecurities to admit that I felt that my entire existence itself was of no consequence. I was utterly, completely existentially invalid. I felt consigned to a state of perpetual inconsequentiality. It wasn't that I wanted to die, because that wouldn't have helped. I wanted to cease to exist, as if I had never been.

I thought I had hit bottom before, but I now realized that there is not a final bottom. Life is not for the faint-hearted, I surmised. From the heights of the potential fulfillment of my dearest dream I once again dove into self-invalidating pain that was like the sting of a thousand scorpions.

My desolation was complete. I screamed to the mountains, "Take this pain, take my attachment to this idealized man, and take my attachment to an idealized self. Help me to be me and to love myself as I am."

In answer to my entreaties, unexpected joy engulfed me for no external reason whatsoever. It was Love without a reason, and unreasonable love. Miraculously, I experienced life itself as a romance with God. That quickly, that easily, the pain that could have gone on for days was gone.

My joy continued to unfold day by day. Life was not without its ups and downs and daily challenges, but as soon as I felt the challenge, a solution would present itself in the form of some small miracle. I continued to be ruthlessly honest in scrutinizing my motivations to see which ones were fear-based or self-centered, coming from my little "I." It became easier and easier to acknowledge these motivations as well as my mistakes—without any judgment. I began to feel truly loved and supported as I experienced Love's presence in every action throughout my day.

In the midst of this miraculous entwinement with the Divine, I experienced a radiant inner self who had been waiting to be revealed. I experienced my own magnificence to such a degree that I fell in love with this part of myself. While I had experienced many extraordinary and sometimes prolonged glimpses of this over the years, I was now in a full-blown experience. I dared to view myself from outside, and saw perhaps for the first time what others saw.

In the face of this startling perception, it became painfully sobering that I had been fighting a life-long battle through thick walls of self-hatred and self-perceived ugliness. I had never been able to understand why anyone would find me beautiful or desirable. It wasn't until now that I could experience this degree of self-love. In this moment, I loved myself the way I imagined I would feel toward the most exquisite lover or him towards me. I loved myself the way I loved God.

This revelation simplified life. I only needed to be myself. It wasn't a matter of giving or serving or doing or fixing. Allowing my own radiance to emanate forth was all that was needed.

I could not find a word or phrase for this radiance; nothing quite described its quality. But I knew I was feeling my own self, which was an experience beyond description. At the same time, my mind sought to define what I needed to do with this radiance. I thought of being of service, or being a vehicle, an instrument, or an agent of the Light. I thought of being a spiritual teacher, an emissary, transmitting the Light, or emanating one's presence. I had already identified with these concepts. Now, none of them captured the essence of what I was sensing. It was a concept beyond words, so I let go of explaining in favor of experiencing.

Gently my heart began to open. I was in a state of grace with no effort. Laughter and joy were present throughout the day. Paradoxically, there was both purpose and purposelessness to all I did. I had never felt so soft, so surrendered, so nakedly open, and yet so full all at once.

"God, whatever you would have of me is what I want. My heart is with you and my life is filled with grace. Show me your heart's desire and it my desire, too."

The brilliance of what seemed to be a billion suns illuminated me and I felt the Divine Mother presence come into me. She cradled the whole planet in her gentle hands. She wept tears of sorrow that people throughout the world had not yet wept for themselves. With a heart of compassion she enveloped humanity in her tenderness.

"The world is in such pain; let me help to ease it. Let my Love flow through you like a river into the world. Their pain is my pain and they are hurting badly. Let me love them, touch them, and help them know joy. Hold your hands like a cup and receive my energy."

I cupped my hands and felt her waves of light and warmth filling the container. I was wondering what to do with this energy when I found my hands moving, spontaneously pouring it from the cup out to the people of the world. Tears of gratitude streamed down my face for the great compassion I felt from the selflessly giving heart of the Mother.

Even with all of these blissful frequencies coursing through me daily, I was wondering why I was still not in the kind of relationship I wanted. I decided to find out what unconscious walls of defense were obstacles between me and other people.

I began to ask the friends and ex-lovers in my life what prevented them from loving me more. The answers ranged from envy to fear of rejection, fear of being loved conditionally by me, to feeling like I wouldn't receive their love. I absorbed the feedback as helpful, but a terrible ache persisted in my heart.

There was one student back in Florida for whom I inexplicably felt immense hatred. I had been dealing with this by trying to shut periodic thoughts of her out of my mind. This had done nothing to reduce my ill feelings towards her. As I sat quietly,

I saw that she represented a part of me that I was still rejecting, hating, and judging as unworthy of love—even after all of the transformational experiences I had undergone in which I thought I had accepted every dark corner of my psyche unconditionally. I decided to take her into my heart, despite my feelings of dislike for her.

I realized that anyone I had not been able to embrace with love was a piece of myself that I had been judging as unlovable. I had rejected these newly discovered parts as well as the people who represented them as a way of holding the darkness at bay. I was, in effect, pushing away the reflection I could not tolerate instead of taking these rejected parts of myself into my own heart.

As I drew the woman I had hated into my heart, a small ball of light formed there. I then brought all of my deepest loves into my heart, and the ball of light began to grow. Soon it grew into a huge golden orb in my heart.

Later that day this woman inexplicably called for a session, and instead of the hatred, I felt great compassion for her. We had a caring session in which she was able to drop some of the attitudes for which I had found greater acceptance.

After the session, the intensity of light within the orb began to grow until the pressure was so great that it exploded. I remembered Gabriella telling me that she had a dream that one day there would be an explosion in my heart. When it actually happened, this explosion created a wide-open space where there had been self-protection before. Love came coursing through like a powerful river flowing in all directions at once.

Soon a drilling sensation began in my forehead that pierced through into the middle of my head and went up through the top. As it pierced the crown, a lotus blossom opened on top of my head and I seemed to disappear into colorlessness. Rays of light shot out all around and a gentle peace washed over me.

"Welcome into me, God. I want you to feel safe and at home in my heart. I don't want you to feel judged, rejected or condemned. I know that pain. You can rest at home in my heart.

"I want my heart to be welcoming and beautiful so that you seek it out. I want my heart to be a safe haven for you, a shelter from the storm. I want my heart to be where you choose to be. Please enter— the door is open wide. I welcome you in.

"I've been gone from you too long and I ask your forgiveness. You are my heart, my soul and my very existence itself. You are everything to me. You are truly my beloved."

the bridge across dimensions

One of the people I had called in doing my survey about my defenses was my mother. We cleared the air and regained our close relationship. She was once again my best friend and confidant. It was hard to have her 3,000 miles away but we spent a lot of time on the phone to make up for the distance. On October 25, 1995, my father's birthday, I received a shocking call from her. She told me she had been diagnosed with inoperable pancreatic cancer and had only three months to live.

My mother had been complaining of abdominal pains for months and I had known there was something amiss with her, but I never thought it would be this. I panicked. If my mother died, my whole world would collapse.

When my mother and I had finished talking, I hung up the phone in a numb, befuddled state.

After a while I came to my senses enough to remember to ask Spirit for help. I received a strong
message that I needed to find a clear and powerful
place in order to gain perspective.

Shamuki and I left the house and climbed a nearby mountain peak. Once there I fell to my knees in
the dirt sobbing, "I feel completely helpless, please
show me the way. I want my mother to live. If that
is possible, please, let it be so. If it is her time to go,
help me to accept this and find peace. How can I
use this crisis for her healing and the awakening of
others as well?"

Through the fear and tears a vision began to form.
It was a vision of a Call to Healing, a network of
Light to help not only my mother but everyone
everywhere in need of support. I thanked Spirit
for this revelation and Shamuki and I went home.
I immediately sat down and drafted a message.

The message spoke of who I was, my mother's illness and my vision of an awakening and healing
not only for her but also for humanity. I asked people to join in on Sunday, November 19th at noon
EST for five minutes. During this time we would

all send love and blessings to the world and ask for the healing we each needed.

I jumped into action and spent the next ten days in a faxing and phoning frenzy all over the world. Within a short time a network of light spread by word-of-mouth all over the world until my anticipated hundreds turned into an estimated fifty thousand, according to my assistant's calculations based on the reports that came in. I was astounded by the powerfully caring response.

The day of the world healing arrived with a sense of expectancy. I had joined my family in Connecticut and we gathered at my parents' newly rented home. At fifteen minutes before noon, we piled onto the large bed in which my mother was propped up by pillows against the headboard. My father and I cradled her like bookends, one on each side, while my sisters and brother gathered around her.

At five minutes before noon we began to prepare. One by one we spoke our intention for my mother's healing, our own healing, and the healing of the world. At noon, a brilliant but gentle light began to fill the room. I sensed my mother's parents in spirit drift in to hold her. I saw a big heart of energy take its place in the center of our family circle. The light began to intensify and I noticed the room filling with angels, Archangels, Ascended Masters and extraterrestrials. We were being infused with an exquisitely pure and radiant Love, which was palpable to us all.

I glanced down at my left hand, which was gently resting on my mother's abdomen above the pancreatic tumor. I saw what appeared to be the hand of God reaching through my hand into my mother's body to illuminate her darkness with a brilliant light. I watched as my mother drifted out of her body and had a vision. Gradually, while she was held in this reverie, a deep peace began to descend upon all of us as we awaited her response. After a while, my mother opened her eyes and said, "I feel I'm going to make it."

"What were you dreaming?" I asked.

"Oh, funny you should ask. I dreamed that I went to the store to buy a pickle, and I was wondering which way they would slice it."

We all looked at her puzzled. Here she was the focus of thousands of people all over the world and she was dreaming of pickles! A mischievous expression crossed her face, "Did you know that the pancreas is shaped like a pickle? I guess I was dreaming about slicing out the tumor." We all smiled. It was so typical of my mother's earthy, practical humor.

My attention was drawn back to the Light and I felt a presence move through me to deliver beautiful, reassuring messages for each family member present. The messages were received amidst many tears. Then my family turned to me and asked, "What about you, Anamika? What is the message for you?"

I closed my eyes to look and at that moment a large golden white cylinder of light surrounded me like a spotlight. "You are Light." I burst into tears. I understood that to mean that I was that Light already and could let go of any doubt that this was so.

The golden white light filled my heart with a quiet peace I'd never known. I felt touched from deep within. The fear of my mother's death had somehow lifted for the moment. The hand of grace was there comforting me whether she lived or died.

I gazed beyond the circle of my family. I saw seeds of light planted all over the world by the people participating in this Call to Healing. Silently, I gave thanks to those whose hearts were open and willing as tears of gratitude spilled from my heart. I looked over at my mother. Her face had relaxed into a deep peace. She said, "For the first time, I can actually imagine that I could heal." I knew that this was true. She could if she wanted to. If she didn't want to, at least she could now release herself peacefully.

When I returned to California I was challenged to embrace the two greatest extremes I could image: the crushing pain of my mother's potential death and the exquisite beauty of the infinite Love with which I was entwined. I was bouncing back and forth like a rubber ball between the two different realities. Of necessity, I had to learn peace in the eye of the storm, while the winds of inner and outer change blew furiously. This lesson in equilibrium reached a fevered pitch on New Year's Eve.

There were unusual colored rings around the moon and an eerie feeling in the air. The night sky was clear except for four elongated streaks of purple clouds. An air of expectancy filled my mountain home as a small group of us gathered for Sakkara. The drumming began and the energies of Sakkara filled the room.

As if on cue, the winds began to whip up from the ocean through the canyon and swirled violently at 80 mph around the mountain. The windows were rattling and off in the distance were explosions of light as generators blew out. One by one the homes in the canyon and along the ocean went dark. The lights in my home flickered on and off and finally blew out.

Sakkara's loving energies held us peacefully in the eye of the storm while the winds raged around us. Trees were blowing down, hitting power lines and bursting into flames off in the distance. While it was too close for comfort, some how I knew we were not in danger. Not only were the lights out, but the phones went dead and the whole town came to a standstill.

The elements were announcing a shift and taking out the old with them. It seemed like thousands of years were being cleared away, preparing space for the new. I knew that in the immediate years to come, we would need to be at peace in the eye of the storm while the winds of change roared all around us. I closed my eyes and breathed a sigh of relief as the gentle arms of Spirit rocked us in safety and peace.

I wondered what such a powerful forecast of change would bring into my life. I feared that it would have to do with my mother. Though my family put a lot of energy into my mother's healing, she was not taking charge of her own well-being. This was a sharp contrast to her hopeful state of mind after the Call to Healing. She was not getting better. It felt like we were dragging her along, trying to convince her to take care of herself and to live. At times, I felt completely incapacitated by the fact that my mother might actually die. This realization made the lack of a partner in my life even more painful.

I had to let go and to learn to accept that things were out of my control. I was mistakenly expecting the Creator to make my life better and that is not how things work. As I saw the unrealistic expectations I was placing on an external God, I was able to really be in the moment and not focus on a man or my mother's possible death. The pain lifted and I felt centered once again.

On Valentine's Day, Shamuki and I were hiking in the mountains admiring the beauty of nature. When I arrived at the foot of my driveway, my lower back unexpectedly seized up. I doubled over in pain and was unable to stand upright. I literally crawled up the steep incline of my driveway and managed to stumble into the house. As I was massaging my back to ease the pain my father called to tell me that my mother was failing rapidly. I asked him to put her on the phone.

A thick voice, groggy with painkillers, that was a pale echo of my mother's usual vibrant tones, weakly greeted me. "I'm dying, Anamika."

"I'm jumping on the next plane. Don't die before I get there," I implored.

"I'll wait for you sweetheart," she assured me.

No wonder my body had seized up! I had allowed myself to hope that she might be healing in spite of herself. That hope made this violent blow even more devastating. Though I was mentally prepared for this eventuality, nothing could have prepared me emotionally. I went back into the state of numb shock I had felt at the time of my mother's first phone call.

Half of me was in my body and the other half was out with my mother who was dwelling more and more in another dimension. I yearned to wake up from this bad dream and return to the joyous life I had been living. My higher self could feel the beauty, power, and opportunity of this transition, and could celebrate my mother's liberation, but my emotional self was devastated beyond description. The reality of her dying was unspeakable and unbearable. It was beyond my ability to cope with or accept what was happening.

In addition to her being my mother—the most primal, life-giving connection—she was also my best friend, trusted advisor, and part of the foundation of my being. We shared everything and understood each other without words. She saw me through the eyes of her soul, despite many years of rough patches. We had persisted through working out the glitches, and all the while she had been there loving me, boosting me up, cheering me on. Ultimately, she had supported my path and understood my motives.

My mother was a powerful, highly intuitive and gifted woman, who spread love to those around her—yet she had a difficult personality, as well. She was of the utmost importance to me, despite her overbearing traits. During her illness, our connection had deepened as she became more vulnerable and open.

During my previous visit with her I had sat hour after hour holding her ailing, cancer-ridden body. I looked into her eyes while she was awake and asleep. There was nothing left to say or feel but, "I love you, Mom, beyond all measure, more than life itself, and I will always be with you."

I had silently communicated, "I have more work to do here in this world, but I'll join you as soon as I can." She had looked deeply into my soul and repeated to me what she had told me again and again from the day I was born, "How could I ever love anyone more than you?"

All too soon her condition had worsened. Now she was in the hospital and rapidly failing. My child-self wailed and grieved for my mommy and my adult-self held her in my strength as my heart shattered and broke wide open. Whatever traumatic life transitions I had previously experienced paled before the impending death of my mother. Nothing compared.

I saw my attachments to her. They included my inability to let her go, to let her choose her own path in her own way, and my own need for her physical presence. I saw all of these things, but it didn't change the fact that I didn't want to let her go, even though I did want her to be happy and free.

Torn between worlds, I called Joffrey in hopes of some helpful perspective. Yeshua spoke through him with loving reassurance that the matter was out of their hands; it was between my mother and God. He said that if she could let go into the heart of the Spirit of the Universe, then she could be happy and find the Light. He said that there was only a small chance that she would heal in her current body and that she would need my help to make her transition. He reminded me that the love my mother and I shared with each other would be a bridge across the dimensions.

I hung up the phone knowing that ultimately I would have to walk this alone. While Yeshua's words gave me comfort, I still felt pain searing through my heart and soul, tearing me open until my nerves seemed raw and exposed. I felt helpless and vulnerable to the point of wanting to die with her. But I had to find the strength to walk this path without her support; she needed mine.

It all seemed unfair. I had spent forty-three years fighting through the entangled emotions between us. We had shared those years of darkness and now that my life was finally opening into joy, I wanted to share that with her, too. I wanted to experience the fruits of our hard work together. I was finally becoming more real, and I wouldn't be able to share it physically with the one about whom I cared most and who cared most about me.

Until now I had taken her presence for granted, as if she would always be here. I hadn't fully appreciated her nor seen the radiance of her spirit. Despite the bond between us, she had also been so judgmental and controlling that at times my heart had hardened towards her. She hadn't been open to growing, healing and changing. Sometimes the best I had been able to do was to hate her for being the way she was. "Mom, please forgive me for every moment I didn't accept myself and therefore you. Part of me is dying with you and I want a rebirth for both of us."

Images of her birthing me and now me escorting her through her death transition flooded my mind. Death and birth, I reflected silently, it's all the same. "Help me dwell further in true Love. Help my mother know true Love. I want everything for her. Help me let her go. Help me love with a pure heart."

All at once I felt lifted into another dimension where my mother was dwelling. I saw the magnificence of her spirit and that we were eternally connected. I remembered Joffrey's words, "To enter God's heart, you have to let go of everything."

After all of this depth of understanding, it was now time to face the reality of her impending death and walk it through. I put a brace on my ailing back and hobbled to the airport. I flew to my parents' home by the sea in Connecticut. My mother was now home in hospice care.

My father, my siblings and I sat with my mother hour after hour, day after day. She was in and out of consciousness as her breathing became more labored. At night when she awoke in pain and screamed my name I jumped out of sleep and ran to her bedside by the picture window overlooking the ocean. The inky black darkness outside felt like it was inside of me. The only light was the illumination that would appear on her face. Periodically, she opened her eyes, smiled weakly at me and then drifted off again.

My family held vigil, suspended beyond time. We functioned as one organism, taking turns holding her, crying in each other's arms, offering food to each other, and talking in hushed tones. Not one element was out of place. It was impossible to miss the elegant orchestration at work.

Although most of my mother's spirit wasn't in her body anymore, the small part that still remained was experiencing great pain despite the ever increasing doses of morphine. She was clearly transitioning. I called Joffrey again for help and this time it was Merlin who came to my aid.

He gave me very specific instructions about telling Joffrey to light three candles of different colors and what to write underneath each one. Merlin disappeared in haste thrusting Joffrey forcefully back into his body. Joffrey came to with a groan. When I alerted him to the situation, he said he would consult with Merlin again to do the magic as the situation called for his power. He said he would instruct Merlin to call me when it was done. I agreed and went in to see my mother.

As I entered the room, everyone else mysteriously decided to take a break, leaving me alone with my mother. I breathed a sigh of relief that I didn't have to explain Merlin's magic, and I lay down next to her according to his instructions. Very soon I felt myself swirling and lifting as I was pulled through the dimensions with my mother. I lost consciousness and awoke with a jolt half an hour later as I was coming back into my body. I immediately reached for the phone by the bedside and called my answering service. Merlin's familiar voice had left a message. It was comforting that he had been involved in this process and I was still hoping against hope she would choose to live. He informed me that their part of the work was now done, without telling me what it had entailed. They said that whatever transpired next was between my mother and the Creator.

Later that day I felt myself being pulled out of my body again. I ran back into her room to be with her. For the second time, when I arrived the other family members mysteriously departed. My mother and I were lifted through the dimensions once again and arrived at the threshold of a door to the Light. I was instructed to wait while she was received into the arms of the Supreme Love. Waiting outside the door that my mother had entered, I could feel the choice that she had made, but I hoped against hope that it wasn't true.

When I returned to my body, I opened my eyes. As I held her, she stirred and opened her eyes. She looked at me and spoke clearly but from very far away, "Anamika, I want to go home."

The decision had been made. Inwardly I crumbled while I mustered my courage to say, "I know, Mom. You're free to go. I'll be with you forever."

She looked at me again from far away and simply whispered, "I know. I love you forever. You are my true lover."

I knew what she meant by those words as she spoke to me from eternity. Then she drifted off again as her spirit pulled out and far away. She had a luminous look on her face again.

My mother's lungs were filling with fluid and it was increasingly difficult for her to breathe. I sensed that she was in the last phase and was pulling out very quickly now. We brought in an overnight nurse who happened to be Hungarian, from the old country, as was my mother's mother. On the surface this seemed like coincidence, but I knew that synchronicity was at work. The midwife for her departure was from the same land as her mother, who was the midwife of her arrival into this world.

I asked the nurse to speak to my mother in Hungarian telling her that she loves her and to let go into the Light. Seeing her unbearable pain, for her sake, we all sincerely wanted her to let go. As the nurse spoke in Hungarian, my mother turned her head to the nurse and weakly reached her arms toward her as if reaching for her own mother. She relaxed and drifted farther off.

We were all gathered around her bed. My father was holding her head, I was pressed against her side holding her hand and my two sisters and brother were similarly positioned around the bed holding her. Her breathing began to slow and become shallower. Her hands began to get white and grow cold as she was pulling the rest of her life force out of her body.

Her lungs were rapidly filling with liquid while her body was fighting to hold on, struggling to survive, and trying to get air. We gently encouraged her to relax and let go. While it was painful to watch the physical struggle, there was a mystical beauty about it all. I could sense that her spirit was far away. She gasped the word "air," then gradually her breathing lightened until she let go.

She was gone. My body went into spasms and nearly fell to the floor as my mother pulled stagnant veils off of me and took them with her. She was setting us both free. As the veils tore loose, the psychic pain was excruciating and emotional floodgates sprang open. It was done. She was going where she had chosen to be. Finally, a gentle peace began to spread through my body; it was all okay.

Drawing away from her bed, our arms formed a circle around each other into which we poured our tears, our grief, and our pain. We sobbed from the depths of our souls, while in a chorus saying, "Mom, keep heading for the Light." Our love was the bridge she crossed into the heart of the Divine.

I was relieved, yet grief-stricken, and held in a protective cocoon of anesthesia-like fog. I knew it would wear off at the rate I could handle. We were walking as if in a dream. Space and time had ceased to exist. All I could sense was the most immediate now.

Completion ceremonies arose spontaneously and each was beautiful, from the heart. The first one occurred the day after her crossing in a dense bank of fog. My father and siblings and I walked out onto the rocks toward the sea, her red Valentine's roses from eight days before in hand. There was one stem for each person. One by one we gently plucked the red petals and tossed them into the ocean while crying our hearts out. We spoke to her of our love, blessing her on her journey, and encouraging her onward. We embraced as a unified group as the petals floated away into the surreal mist.

As always, the elements were in harmony with the mood. The day she crossed there was dense, heavy atmospheric pressure and oppressive overhanging clouds. After she crossed the skies opened up and it poured, mirroring our tears. Then we were fogged in. The ceiling remained low, but the rain lifted as we put her body in the ground. With white roses this time we spoke to her again, one by one placing the flowers on the wooden box before we shoveled in the dirt. One of her friends had brought four chocolate roses wrapped in red tinsel in honor of her fondness for chocolate.

We invited friends and family to come together later that day to celebrate her life. The sky was beginning to lighten slightly. Holding hands in a large circle, we spoke of her life, told stories, laughed and cried. Her charisma had touched each in a unique way. Such was her gift.

As soon as the stories were completed there was an audible sigh and we were lifted higher. At that moment the sun burst through the cloudbank for the first time in days. The sky looked like my heart, gray and dense but with rays of light bursting through. We still walked as if in a dream.

Exhausted from the whole ordeal, I lay down to rest and asked God to show me the way. As if a switch were activated, a wellspring, like an eternal fountain of Love began to circulate in my heart. My only desire was to let it flow outward, spilling over and blanketing all with grace.

"Ah, this is altruistic love," I thought. "How bittersweet." I was elated and sad. "How ironic," I mused, "to have to lose my dearest love to experience more. How true that love is letting go."

I could sense more veils being pulled off gently as I was moving through a tunnel of gray mist. This was my transition, my mother's parting gift. She had birthed me into this world and I had birthed her into the next dimension. She was carrying me there with her. She and I had birthed and mothered each other for lifetimes.

I could sense that with her departure from this form my new life would begin. Together we were journeying further into the heart of the Beloved and were united in our love.

exposing the dictator

In the days after my mother's death, I had much to understand and a need to recover. Yeshua helped me understand the process she was undergoing—from the initial exhilaration of freedom to holding onto old earthly beliefs that still had a charge. I could sense her being at peace, held by soothing energies but she had not been one to willingly face her dark side. Since she had not consciously chosen to do so while in life, I could sense her getting to face fear after fear now as a result of going through such an intense change of dimensions. As she faced them, she relinquished them one by one and came to greater peace.

I was able to track her in each stage of her process and stayed in close contact through it all. I was grateful that I was facing my darkness now so I didn't have to wait until physical death to dwell in joy and peace. That more exalted state was available to us now without having to wait to die. We could shift dimensions of consciousness even while in the same body.

For weeks after my mother's crossing, I felt myself outside of space and time. It was an odd sensation. While in this detached state, I sensed more veils being removed and I scoured clean every bit of internal debris I could find by recognizing and finding compassion for each piece. I couldn't relate to anything that was happening on Earth from world events to the neighbor's problem with termites.

I was aware that I was further letting go of my life as it had been and getting to see more clearly that my old ways didn't work. In the context of that admission, I could forgive myself for having believed in and engaged in some twisted perspectives. I had been driven by survival fears, and had emotionally engaged in all kinds of manipulation, selfishness and seduction. I realized that freedom would come not from elimination of my dark, but from compassion born of its illumination.

Like my mother coming to peace with her dark side, it was time for me to do more of the same. Even though I had been looking at it from many angles and accepting it at ever-deeper levels, I had still persisted in fearing it and trying to control it. When I thought about control, suddenly a strange, ill-at-ease feeling crept up. Something inside me was rebelling. I was sick of striving for perfection and trying to do everything right so that I could "ascend." I had been here before. I had experienced moments of acceptance of the whole of me. Yet I saw that I had not yet fully accepted some inner darkness that I thought I had embraced.

So, instead of trying to do it right, I shouted to the mountains, "You know what, God? If I can't tell you the complete and honest truth about how I feel, and if you can't see what's really in my heart anyway, then we have a severe problem in our relationship.

"I am sick and tired of trying to make myself feel some altruistic, ascended way. I am just going to tell you the way I actually feel. This isn't my highest wisdom or most elevated perspective; it's just the emotional garbage at the moment, so here it is: In this moment I don't give a damn about serving! In fact, I don't care about anything or anyone right now.'

It felt good to make these unabashed, honest statements, so I persisted: "I want to be in control, I want to dictate what's what. In fact, I don't want to give myself to you at all. I want you to bend to MY will In fact, I'M God!"

The dictatorial voice inside of me became forcefully vicious and persisted. "I want you to be miserable and suffer. I don't want you to even be able to breathe. I don't care about your happiness. I don't care about anybody else's either! I am cold-hearted and don't care about anyone or anything." The dispassionate part of me saw quite clearly that this inner dictator was deriving immense negative pleasure from this obstinate, vindictive attitude.

It became startlingly clear that this dictator was blocking my heart from opening further. I had been attempting to force myself to be wide open and caring despite this hold-out place that didn't give a damn about anything but itself, and didn't even care about itself much either.

I let the dictator loom large so I could see it. Then a gentle, soothing voice came from the deepest recesses of my being. "All I want is for you to be happy." This genuine caring caught the dictator so off guard that "he" burst into tears. "I have never felt loved unconditionally, just because I exist," this aspect of me said.

I redirected my words back to God. "I never felt that you wanted me to be happy either. I have felt that you just want me to be of service, and to do the Great Work. I've been resisting because I never felt like you cared about me just for me." The dictator felt so loved because someone was considering his happiness, that he left center stage. In his place was a gentle voice in the center of my heart. "I care about your happiness, and your control has been in the way of you receiving my love."

"All I care about is being happy."

"Let that desire go too. There's something beyond what you imagine as happiness. You don't yet even know the fullness of what you can experience, so don't limit yourself in any way."

I replied from the most delicately tender open heart: "What I truly want is to feel our hearts together."

Suddenly a profound joy exploded in my heart. "Oh, I feel at one with you in my heart! It's so gentle and sweet." Unexpectedly, I experienced excitement about the unknown instead of the usual fear.

I had feared God as something outside of and bigger than me. I had attempted to stay in control, to brace against the punishment, judgment, and deprivation that I thought was coming from God. I didn't know that it was me who was doing all that to myself and then projecting it outward. I began to see that it was my own control that was limiting my happiness and not some external God who could either limit it or grant it.

I began to see that all the while God had been helping me lift beyond the limitations of what I thought I wanted to something I couldn't yet see. I boldly proclaimed, "From this place of trust, I let go of control. I will happily follow whatever our hearts want, because that's so much better than anything I could arrange for myself through the limited perceptions of control."

I had never expected to be plunked into my heart in this way. I felt Love dwelling deep within it and I was dwelling in the heart of my Beloved.

But different steps of this union always did occur in the most unexpected ways. As I surrendered control, facing the dictator became the liberator. I was dancing in a fluid, mutable entwinement. The yearning for anything outside of myself dissolved as the inner marriage was occurring more fully between the lover and the beloved. I experienced our oneness to a greater degree than at any time before.

Shells of protection cracked open to reveal a mangled, wounded part. I asked, "Where is my lover?" God replied: "I am your lover. Why are you rejecting me?" I gave my mangled heart to God who received it with gratitude. An indescribable sweetness filled me. Once again I felt that unbearably beautiful intimacy I had been craving since childhood.

A tender mist enveloped me and within it I sensed a luminous presence. It magnetically drew me forward, pulling me into itself. As I yielded, I sensed that this was the process my mother had experienced in her transition. Held in this Love, I understood why her choice to surrender to it was inevitable. The world held no sway; this Love was her home, and home to us all.

It became evident that this attraction had always been present. It was my own limitations in receiving its magnitude that had disrupted the flow. It had always been there inviting me inexorably forward. As I dissolved into its tender embrace, paradoxically, I was still me, and also We. This was not ordinary love.

I understood again my mother's choice. After she had crossed over, I was aware of her doing a review of her life. In near death experiences, many have reported that their life flashes before their eyes. A similar review was now occurring for me as if I were physically dying. For hours I watched scenes from my life in my mind's eye as if on video. I cried for hours as each scene passed by, saying goodbye to what had been and feeling the loss of my life as I had known it.

There were childhood scenes of my mother holding me. I would never feel her physical warmth again. There were scenes from relationships with lovers to whom I had said goodbye.

As the review came to a close, I saw several of the same scenes again and this time there was no pain. The charge was gone. The scenes were simply memories, filed in the memory bank of life. I attempted to see the future and it did not exist. I looked back into the past. It was complete. Sitting in the vastness of now, with the past released and no future in sight, I breathed a sigh of relief.

"I have nothing left to give you but this self-doubt."

"Yes, you do have something more to give me; it's your trust."

These words slammed me against a wall of hardness within me. I began to cry as fear clutched my heart. "I give you my trust. Please take it quickly and don't let me take it back." As I said this, fear of entrapment and suffocation loomed large, threatening to reverse my decision. My lungs tightened making it nearly impossible to breathe.

"Despite this fear, I commit. Don't let me leave you. Don't let me pull away, walk away, or take my love away. Hold me close. Help me forgive my self-serving nature and instead surrender into Love."

I felt myself expanding beyond the fear of entrapment and through a doorway into a new awareness. "I know that my fear has been blocking my fuller union with you and therefore with other people too." Then shockingly I heard myself speak in a low, clear and steady voice: "You're the one I want to marry. I am ready to commit."

This commitment was occurring at a deeper level this time than when I first made these vows. I saw that it was never once and for all. With this choice to recommit yet again, a gentle peace descended.

CHAPTER 24

heart flame

My peaceful state did not last long enough. It seemed like everything was wrong. Why did I have to do this alone? My body felt sick, my emotions a mess. I was miserable, bored and despairing.

Every day I'd wake up and the dark hole seemed to consume me. Where were those moments of not so long ago when everything felt so right with life and I was at peace with the world? I could re-member those moments but I couldn't feel them.

I called Joffrey and went on a long rant into the phone to Miriam. "The constant non-arrival of my soul mate makes me feel there is something wrong with me. No matter how much I adhere to the path, it never happens. This lack of intimacy makes me feel like I am starving to death and that it's okay that I get sacrificed. It doesn't seem to matter that it is taking all of this time. My deepest pain never gets fully lifted and I always just get my own insecurities shoved in my face. I can't take any more! My powerlessness makes me feel even more hopeless because there is nothing that I can do. I must do this and be like that and I can't do any of it. I don't have the ability. I can't love myself or make myself receive it. I don't enjoy the process. Right now I hate it all! I don't believe that I will ever be cherished no matter how hard I try. I cannot change or fix myself any more. I'm not the kind of person who is so humble that I'm grateful for every little thing and I'm sick of trying to make myself other than who I am. I am in the agony of emptiness and I'm not a good sport about it. I admit that I do often experience Light, but it's not consistent enough to make me happy. Without Love, nothing else matters or is important to me. The outer world doesn't even exist for me right now. All I am seeing is the connection and disconnection. I feel totally incapable of anything right now and I'm starving to death! I don't want a life here if I'm not going to be personally happy, and the only thing that makes me happy is that Love. I don't have the faith needed for this. I am nowhere! I feel like I'm going to die right now. I'm suffocating." I felt like I had entered the bowels of hell.

Wracked with sobs, I began gasping for breath. "I need help, I can't breathe. Don't leave me, I need you."

Suddenly, I felt God's loving presence holding me, filling me and soothing me. I began to relax.

I had felt victimized by my situation and was not yet at a stage of development of true ownership. I couldn't yet see that I was pushing away the Love from within and from others who wanted to give it. I couldn't yet admit that I was causing my own pain. One hundred percent ownership was a large pill to swallow.

In this early stage of taking ownership I was saying, "You hurt me." I was riddled with blame of myself and others. "You don't love me. You scared me. You're not giving me what I want. I'm not good enough and no one else is either, so I'll push Love away while saying it isn't there."

Then later, in learning to take ownership I moved on to, "Maybe there is something in common with all of the situations in which I find myself, in which I feel the same way." What do all of these situations have in common? Me! What am I believing about Love? When I say it isn't there, what am I doing with my energy? What am I believing about myself and my own worth?

Even later, taking one hundred percent responsibility without blame sounded something like this: I create my own reality without exception, no fine print. This was especially hard to swallow in cases of people being terribly mistreated. But when I allowed for no exceptions, and no blame, I could recognize and acknowledge what core beliefs of mine were creating every situation. Then I could bring forgiveness and compassion to myself for believing them, and choose to open into more empowering perspectives beyond my limited beliefs that created each situation. As I tell the truth about what I'm currently believing and then bring compassion, I change.

In taking ownership, I also learned to ask which part of me is speaking? For example, when a young part feels powerless, she tries everything to find power. She tries to take control so as to find 'power over' and become 'more powerful than...' Eventually I was secure enough within myself to allow this child to actually feel her powerlessness as a beautiful emotion, and not misinterpret it to mean there is something wrong and I won't survive. I learned to soften into all feelings, even fear and powerlessness, rather than struggling and fighting against them.

Feeling pure emotion without a big story attached brings relief. For example, through the relief of feeling powerlessness I accessed a new level of real power that is entirely different than my child looking for her version of power. I discovered that feeling the powerlessness of the small part opened me into the power of the bigger me.

I had identified very thoroughly with this limited identity, this finite self, that I thought was me. I had thought that I needed to be some wonderful persona to feel worthy. I had thought that just being my real self was not enough because it included darkness and imperfections. I had believed that the vulnerable openness of admitting all parts of me would be the death of me. Even though I kept learning the same lesson over and over, each time I did so more deeply and completely –it doesn't happen once and for all times.

In trying to project a shiny image, instead of being transparent and authentic, I had inadvertently polished my arrogance and pride. I had forced a separation from my natural emotions to try to be something more. Ironically, it was that the very attempt not to feel bad that was causing me so much pain. When I could see it, I could forgive and grow beyond saying it was my fault.

The impulse to protect and defend moves in the opposite direction of the vulnerability needed to let go of defenses in order to open into further realness. Paradoxically, one needs to be strong and safe enough internally to allow for this kind of undefended vulnerability, which is a strength, not a weakness.

As I became more vulnerably open, I could sense that I was limitless beyond what I could imagine. In contrast to what's infinite, our identity is very small. As I was becoming more trusting of my infinite nature, I found myself moving my God ring back to the ring finger of the left hand. But, it ended up on the middle finger instead. "Almost but not quite," I heard myself say aloud. "It's you that I want, and I've been projecting it on a man."

I suddenly felt very shy, like a one-year-old little girl who wanted to marry her daddy. I had buried that little girl under heaps of shame. "Of course you want your daddy," I reassured her.

I brought my attention back to the present. "I want to marry you, God, will you have me?" I pulled my God ring off of my middle finger and held it above my ring finger.

"Are you ready now?" a patient voice inquired. "Yes!" I responded sliding the ring down my ring finger. Piercing light and ecstatic Love exploded in my heart. Sensations and emotions opened that I didn't even know existed. Entwined in the arms of my Beloved I heard God's tender voice say, "Do I please you as your lover?" I melted. "Please me? This is the most exquisite love-making I have ever experienced!"

An ironic chuckle arose within me. "You know," I thought, "the conclusion of my search is this: I still don't know intellectually if God exists and is everything, but I don't care one iota. I am now able to say, "Yes, you are for real, forever, and all things. The reason I know this is because I am helplessly, utterly, unreasonably and limitlessly in love. And when I feel this way, I know that I am this Love."

I had crossed a threshold into the heart of my Beloved. I was wide open in a sea of infinite possibility. A space gently opened in the center of my heart. I looked inward and saw there a beautiful shining jewel. Inside the jewel was a light, a heart flame. It was emitting a radiance so bright and pure that tears of joy slid down my cheeks. "Ah," I thought, "This is who I truly am. Each one of us is a unique, magnificent jewel, emanating our radiance."

Within this context the highs and lows could come and go, but they seemed small and irrelevant. I began to trust life as it unfolded. I was at peace and calm in a way that was nothing like what I had I expected or experienced in the past. Once again, I got to throw away all of the images I had held of myself, of enlightenment, and of my future life. All that was real was to simply be in the unfolding that was happening now.

One by one I took the dreams I had constructed for my life and tossed them like imaginary rose petals into the sea near my house in Montecito. It was like the completion ceremony my family had performed when my mother crossed over. The very largest petals were the dreams of a future, unnamed man. I watched as the mist surrounded the petals and the waters gently carried them away.

This radiance persisted, and as it did I found myself becoming enraged. I was enraged that I had never believed that I had the right to exist simply as myself. I was enraged that I had been referencing life and God outside of myself. I was enraged that I had never felt that my existence was valid.

As I dared to claim my validity, my own life force surged through me with such sweetness. In this current, I experienced not only a personally intimate union with All, but the joy of expressing myself freely as me. In this sweetness, I realized that I was not searching for a man. I already had many beautiful men in my life. I had been searching for the freedom to be fully myself—shadow and light.

Over the next few weeks a cocoon formed around me. Burrowing deeply inside, the outer world dropped away to such a degree that I could barely even speak. Oddly, my physical body seemed to be dying. My skin turned gray and my mane of dark curls fell out in handfuls. At first I was horrified, then I jokingly referred to my ailment as Old Soul's Syndrome. I realized that even my physical body had to be remade anew.

Gabriella would check in on me often, which was comforting. Yet, I needed to trust in this unknown process. Instead of doing my own breathing, I felt existence itself breathe me in and out of Creation. In that surrender, I would lie on the couch and open to the breath of life coming into me. It felt as if something other than my finite self was breathing me back into life. I began to feel as if my DNA was being recalibrated and re-encoded to a higher frequency. Each rise in vibration allowed me more access to multidimensional awareness.

The dying intensified and I revisited the symptoms of childhood sicknesses. I became violently ill, as if a plug had been pulled. I was drained as all of my vitality was being utilized in this process. Physically exhausted, I moved from the couch to the chair and back to the couch again. These short trips across the room required every bit of my energy. Dishes piled up in the sink and dust settled throughout the house as I focused on this transformation.

I came to understand that I was reincarnating in the same physical body without literally dying and having to come back again. My old life was complete and the old programs were dropping away. My only purpose now was being and becoming. It seemed I was living in a still point as this occurred because nothing outside of this zone existed as I allowed myself to be made anew.

This zero point lasted for three days. On the morning of the fourth day I sprung awake at 5 a.m. full of life energy and joy. My body was ravaged by my spiritual ordeal but I saw that I now had the resources to begin the process of rebuilding.

Surprisingly, my life until that moment seemed like a past life of my present self. It was as if I had lived that whole life in a different dimension of being. That life had been a struggle to get somewhere, and to become who I now knew myself to be. I wasn't reaching outside of myself with some thought of a soul mate. There was no angst. Life in this new dimension was beginning to unfold as harmonious and splendid.

I felt I had the Love in my life for which I had searched and it was growing rapidly every day. There was nothing to prove anymore. Being in the Love was all that mattered. This Love was sweet beyond compare. Some days it was passionate, even highly erotic as it surged through my body. Other days I smiled and laughed at the play of it all. Tears of gratitude ran down my cheeks for the incomparable beauty and almost unbearable intimacy of its embrace. Truly, there was no way to describe it. It was a passion beyond all comprehension.

As I grew more sure-footed and trusting of its enduring nature, I was able to let go more deeply into it. Every belief I held about myself, the world, or the nature of reality gently came to my attention so that I could go beyond its limitations. Every story, even the most exquisite ones, got to be seen, held in compassion, and relinquished so that who I was beyond them all could emerge. The only consistency was a constant letting go and opening into further recognition, acceptance and gratitude.

I knew this is what I had come here to do, not for some sense of mission, but because I wanted to. At the same time I was pioneering new territory daily, I was helping guide others ignite their heart flame, too, just through the energy I was starting to embody. There was nothing left to say. All that mattered was that my heart was bursting open ever more day-by-day. I now understood that meeting "the man" would never occur in the way I had imagined. It was a relief to stop projecting old images of what I thought I needed into the future. These images had been thwarting real Love, including in human form, from coming into my life.

As I relinquished these dreams and my stomach clenched, another aspect of who I thought I was and what I thought I wanted was dying. I relaxed into it. All that was needed was to continue to surrender and everything would unfold—better than I could ever imagine.

indescribable lusciousness

During this time of wonderful changes, I spent most of my time lying inert on the couch. The fatigue was still debilitating. As an inspiration to be able to get back on my feet, Gabriella suggested that I watch the film *Dirty Dancing*. It's about a beautiful male dancer and a young woman who knows nothing about dancing but has a strong desire to do so. He trains her and awakens the dancer and the passionate woman within her. The dancing was so beautiful that I cried from my heart as I watched the movie again and again. Drawn into the beauty, I felt a desire to express my body through the dance that was awakening within me.

I had never danced or engaged in any kind of physical training. I was highly trained in spiritual, emotional, and intellectual arenas, but my body was not developed. Although I was still exceptionally weak, I chose to follow my new interest. I dragged myself out of bed to go to an evening of swing dancing. Although I could barely move, I was on the dance floor with the class doing the three basic steps. We repeated a simple combination of steps over and over. Surprisingly, joy welled up inside of me from the beauty of this simple movement.

I loved the dancing, but most of the men couldn't hold a rhythm. Instead of dancing, they clumsily yanked me around the floor. However, I kept returning to class because the ecstasy of the movement sustained me. The fourth week I was dancing with one of those uncoordinated men and was about to quit. "I can't do this anymore! Where is my beautiful male dancer like in the movie?" I wondered to myself. At that moment, an elegant sandy haired, blue-eyed man poked his head in the door. The teacher called out, "Hey, Branden, we need another man. Can you pitch in for the evening?"

Branden consented and began to circulate, dancing with the women who did not have a regular dance partner. When it was my turn to dance with him, a huge grin spread over my face. This man could really dance and something in me just went wild!

I approached him after the class and asked if he was a ballet dancer. He said that indeed he was and had trained in New York for ten years. Since he'd moved to Santa Barbara he had become involved in Ballroom and Latin dancing. He said he could see that I had no training or experience but that it looked like I adored dancing and he'd be happy to show me a few basics.

When I described my life to him, he looked at me as if I had just escaped from an asylum and began to shrink away in fear. I later found out that his family had been sternly and repressively religious. As a result, Branden hated spirituality, healing and anything to do with what my life was about.

Despite Branden's fear, we got together for an evening. Setting the stage with music from *Dirty Dancing* he took me in his arms and began gently moving to the rhythm. I was so weak I could hardly stand, but I found myself dissolving into a pool of ecstasy. I so appreciated his dancing with me that I offered to give him a session. He reluctantly and very skeptically consented.

As Branden sat down on the couch, I suddenly felt what seemed like the hand of God forcefully reach through me into his chest and grab his heart. He spontaneously burst into tears. "Oh! You are real. I was so wrong. I feel the presence of God here."

He began to see his relationship with his family differently and many things began to unravel for him. He received an extraordinary gift of awakening that evening, which made me happy for his sake and for my own because now I could learn to dance.

After a few weeks of exchanging dance lessons for sessions, Branden invited me to go with him to Los Angeles for his weekly lesson in Ballroom and Latin dancing. He wanted me to meet his teacher Patrick Flannigan, a seventy-year-old, redheaded Irishman.

Patrick had owned three dance studios in London, the hub of international Ballroom dancing. He had moved to Southern California because he preferred the climate. I learned that by accreditation, Patrick was one of the very few in the world who had attained so many high degrees.

From my first glimpse of Patrick, I knew I was in the presence of a great dancer and master teacher.

He had unmistakable dignity, poise and grace. I listened as he was explaining to Branden, "Dance is about the freedom of physical form, body flight through space; it's never, never about steps. It's the expression of your own essence through the aesthetics, geometry, and physics of movement. Your body must respond to your intention of beauty. You are an echo of the music and you must dissolve into the sound. Body flight comes from inner stillness. Feel the floor reaching its hands up to you." This man spoke my language. I looked deeply into his eyes and we instantly bonded.

After Patrick showed Branden a few movements he turned to me and said, "Now, what can you do?" I froze, completely paralyzed and humiliated about my broken down body. Shame washed over me for having a physical body at all, no less one that could hardly move. I knew who I was in spirit but I did not know myself in body. All I had was this depleted form that was trying to resurrect itself. I had no idea how to be a human being in physical form or how to express that with any elegance or grace.

Glued to the spot feeling clunky and stiff, Patrick saw that. He took me gently in his arms and began to move. His energy was the most graceful, fluid and free physical movement I had ever experienced. I simply melted into Patrick and surrendered to him the way I surrender to God. He waltzed me around the floor then brought me back, placed me in Branden's arms and motioned, "Off you go."

Branden had been studying dance over a period of 25 years and here I was, in his arms having to do whatever he was doing. I hadn't gone to LA intending to dance at all, but simply to observe the lesson. I clunked my way around the floor, stepping on him, tripping over myself, but somehow survived the lesson.

At the conclusion of the lesson, Patrick took Branden aside for a man-to-man talk. After their talk Patrick approached me, "You are a good dance partner for Branden. Will you do it?" I heard myself blurting out, "Yes, of course," not knowing at all what I was getting myself into. I had harbored no intention of doing anything like this and yet the dream of becoming a beautiful dancer made me joyously happy.

Immediately my concerns arose. "Patrick, I have chronic fatigue, no training whatsoever and Branden is an experienced dancer."

"All the better," Patrick replied, "I'll have no bad mistakes to undo. I'll train you from scratch." I liked his style and warmed up to him even more.

In that moment my life changed course dramatically. Here I was with an experienced ballet dancer and a world-class master teacher. How did I go from the couch to the ballroom in one breath?

When we returned to Montecito, Branden was more than pleased that I had agreed to be his new dance partner. I was in trepidation about the physical exertion and about my capacity to dance. But Branden assured me he would make it easier by being the one to drive to LA. He was tender and supportive, yet it took every ounce of energy to just get Shamuki into the car, drive down to Los Angeles and make it through each hour-and-a-half lesson.

Dancing was magical and beautiful. Yet I found myself frustrated with my body's inability to move easily. All of the self-hatred that I associated with my body came up. "My body is ugly, disgusting, and ungraceful." All of the issues I had worked on spiritually came out again about how revolting it is to be human in physical form. It's great to be open in one's spirit, but not in the body. By contrast, here was Patrick, a living embodiment of elegance and freedom in physical form. I desperately wanted to be like him.

Branden and I increased our lessons with Patrick to three times a week. Then he encouraged me to take ballet as a foundation for Patrick's work, so I began ballet classes the other days of the week in Montecito. Then there was practice with Branden. Within a week's span, I went from lying on the couch with chronic fatigue to being in serious training, dancing several hours a day, seven days a week.

Branden and I became romantically involved, so we spent much happy time together practicing and participating in dance competitions. He took to my work like a duck to water after his initial experience, so we spent much time healing and awakening as well.

I had certainly opened to invite life in. I didn't want to control it and live in fearful resistance. A new phase of life was definitely now beginning, and once again it moved me on, this time to Malibu. Branden and I had a gentle parting of ways, and he eventually found and married a new dance partner.

While I couldn't see where life was leading me, I had learned to accept Love as the great mystery that it is. To enter its embrace, I continually surrendered everything in order to discover its true nature. It has its own wisdom and course beyond all comprehension. The more I aligned with its flow, the more I basked in its sublime embrace, which was exquisite beyond delicious, and the more I understood it as who I am.

This period of time had been the filling of my heart to bursting. I came to trust this Love. It seemed that I was dwelling in the center of existence itself. This feeling of connectedness with All was nourishing and ecstatic.

As Rumi had expressed so well long ago, "Lovers don't finally meet somewhere. They're in each other all along." I didn't finally find Love. It had been in me and who I was all along. In this sacred embrace, indescribable lusciousness was always available in my heart.

CHAPTER 26

then and now

Nearly twenty years have now passed. What has happened in that time? Of greatest significance to me is that I am continually expanding into a new sense of self, playfulness, lightness and freedom.

Gabriella and I remain dear friends but Joffrey and I are no longer in contact. Our parting of ways was painful at the time, but I am forever grateful for the years we spent together so intensely.

I reached a point where I no longer needed his assistance in the same ways. Though this was a frightening transition for me, it proved to be an empowering one as I continued to integrate the wisdom he had offered at ever deeper levels, and discover more of the richness I had within.

Life-changing leaps continue to occur exponentially. One change is that I'm now comfortable with a level of realness and vulnerability that I never could have tolerated or imagined in the past.

And what of my two original, burning issues, the man and the mission, that drove me to such extremes? I'm happy to say I outgrew that framework entirely. I'm relieved that I no longer have a mission! Instead, I adore sitting with people and experiencing the beauty of the dance between us as we open into places we couldn't have imagined. I delight in the miracles that occur as we discover more of ourselves.

And what about that tall, dark haired man with blue eyes that I had thought was my destiny? Well, he never showed up. So, I finally let that image go, along with the notion of "The One." Another huge relief! I was living in the joy of being alive as me.

Then, out of the blue, I began having sensations of a tall man hugging me etherically. Since these sorts of things had gone on throughout my life, I didn't make much of it. But it continued to happen and was extraordinarily sensual.

Several weeks later, after a series of these visitations, I settled into a new house that had an exotic Moroccan flavor. Speaking of a sensual oasis of beauty! It was symbolic of leaving my old life behind opening more into an internal wellspring of lusciousness.

Shortly after the move I was speaking on Skype with the older brother of one of my dearest friends. We had carved out some time together for what was supposed to be a "meaningful" conversation. I had known him for three years and we had spoken periodically. While I had always felt drawn to him in some strange way, and was happy to help shed some light on his concerns, I was certain we were not matched for a relationship.

While we were engaged in a very "serious" conversation on Skype, Maks the Russian refrigerator repairman arrived to fix some loud clanking. What an inopportune moment, I thought. Since Maks couldn't come back later, although annoyed that he was interrupting our "important" conversation, I let him in.

My friend's brother and I watched as Maks struggled to jockey the refrigerator out of its tight corner. Having no success, Maks began consulting with my friend's brother on Skype about how to move the refrigerator. Through the absurdity of the whole situation, we were laughing so hard that suddenly I began to see him in a more real way.

I invited him to come visit my new home to continue our conversation in person. He showed up with a bouquet of colorful flowers. How unexpectedly thoughtful! I also noticed that the flowers he had selected were more vibrant and playful than those I would ordinarily choose.

We had a wonderful but somewhat awkward chat about male/female dynamics. We were both quite uncomfortable with each other. When he was preparing to leave and I hugged him goodbye, currents of energy suddenly opened up between us and it was as if we experienced each other for the first time. When I touched him, I was stunned that he was the exact size and shape of the presence that had been visiting me. Then I also noticed that he had dark hair with blue eyes.

This man did not fit any of the criteria of who I thought I wanted be with, nor did I match his. But we were inexplicably drawn together. Synchronistically, during the exact weeks I had experienced the etheric visits, he had been receiving visitations from a dark haired woman with olive green eyes who was my size and shape.

Slowly, as we began spending some time together, every bit of resistance reared its head and we did everything to push each other away. Yet, somehow, in the process, we kept getting closer. I remembered that spirit had told me twenty years ago that even if I were looking a wonderful man in the eyes I wouldn't recognize him at first. I hadn't believed them. They had been right after all. He was so far outside of my box I couldn't see him, yet he was so right for me even in the places that seemed all wrong.

Being with each other took us both far out of our comfort zones in a powerfully catalytic and happy direction. He was so emotionally present and real, I was squirming with discomfort while secretly delighted. The same was happening for him. Through our mutual honesty and vulnerability, we kept growing closer.

As our defenses began rapidly dropping, we were able to truly see and appreciate each other. We realized that we had both called the other one to us, custom ordered, but neither matched what our minds had conjured up. His beauty and presence were even more than what my mind's laundry list had imagined. But I had never seen these qualities in him before until we both emerged from behind our walls.

After five months of being together, as I was completing this book I sent him a text. "I need a title for the book I'm writing about Love. I want the title to portray something that's not romantic because what I'm describing is different than that and must be experienced to be understood. Any suggestions?"

He could sense how intent I was about finding just the "right" title, which of course was blocking it from flowing. So in his typically earthy humor he texted back, "How about Flying with the Chickens into Love?" Next to his suggested title was an icon of a speckled chicken. I laughed all afternoon every time I thought of the quirky absurdity of his suggestion and marveled at how he always got me unglued when I was taking myself too seriously.

Later that day, his funny title flashed through my mind. It conveyed the unending adventure we experience together that's full of wonderful surprises. So where am I now? I keep choosing loving now, and loving each moment of now. And, if I had to sum up my entire journey in just a few words, I would definitely say that I'm 'Flying with the Chickens into Love!'

Printed in Poland
by Amazon Fulfillment
Poland Sp. z o.o., Wrocław